EMERGING ASIA

Challenges for India and Singapore

EMERGING ASIA

Challenges for India and Singapore

Edited by

N.N. VOHRA

INDIA INTERNATIONAL CENTRE

MANOHAR
2003

First published 2003

ISBN 81-7304-484-8

Published by
Ajay Kumar Jain for
Manohar Publishers & Distributors
4753/23 Ansari Road, Daryaganj
New Delhi 110 002

Typeset by
Kohli Print
Delhi 110 051

Printed at
Lordson Publishers Pvt. Ltd.
New Delhi 110 007

Contents

Preface

The end of the prolonged Cold War era has witnessed a thawing of the beliefs, theologies and policies which had earlier influenced international relations. While the emergence of a new international order does not appear to be on the threshold the past decade and more has seen the infusion of greater vigour in bilateral and multilateral engagements among countries all over the world.

Since India launched its 'Look East' initiative its interactions with her ASEAN neighbours have intensified significantly. Over three years ago, in summer 1999, the India International Centre (IIC) joined hands with the South Asian Studies Programme of the National University of Singapore (NUS) to organize the 'First Singapore–India Colloquium'. This Colloquium, on 'The Management of Globalization', hosted by the National University of Singapore, discussed papers presented by eminent participants on various aspects of the impact of globalization on Singapore and India.

In winter this year (26–27 February 2002) NUS and IIC organized the 'Second India–Singapore Colloquium'. After consultations with Emeritus Professor Peter Reeves, who has been the Coordinator on behalf of the NUS from the commencement of our collaborative relationship and Co-Convenor of the Colloquium, it was agreed that the theme of the Second Colloquium should be 'Emerging Asia: Challenges for Singapore and India' and that the Singapore–India relations would be discussed under three broad heads: Bilateral Issues; Economics and Development; and Security.

The entire Singapore team consisted of eminent academics. Besides Prof. Reeves, who delivered the Keynote Address, seven NUS scholars presented papers on identified subjects. The Indian participants were drawn from varied backgrounds: a senior Professor from the School of International Studies, Jawaharlal Nehru University; a former Indian Ambassador who had enjoyed several tenures in South-East Asia; two economists, one who is serving as Secretary-General, Federation of Indian Chambers of Commerce and Industry and another who is Editor of the *Financial Express*, a national level financial paper; and two Strategic Analysts, one who is the Director of the Institute for Defence Studies and Analyses and another who is a former Director of this Institute and presently a commentator on Strategic Affairs.

The 'Second India–Singapore Colloquium', hosted by IIC, was inaugurated by H.E. Mr. Kwok-Pun Wong, the then High Commissioner for Singapore and Smt. Suryakanthi Tripathi, the then Additional Secretary (South), Ministry of External Affairs, Government of India. Besides the participants on both sides who presented papers we had valuable contributions from Shri Prem Singh, former Indian High Commissioner to Singapore; Prof. Peter Reeves, Co-Convenor of the Colloquium; Shri S.T. Devare, former Ambassador to Indonesia and Secretary, Economic Relations, Ministry of External Affairs; Dr. C. Raja Mohan, Strategic Affairs Editor, *The Hindu*; and Prof. Dipankar Gupta from the School of Social Sciences, Jawaharlal Nehru University, each of whom chaired the various sessions of the Colloquium.

The discussions on the papers presented at the Colloquium contributed to a better understanding of the respective positions, concerns and apprehensions and a broad based identification of the areas of convergence which, if systematically worked upon, could significantly enlarge the existing level of cooperation between the two countries and beyond. Besides leading to certain hard-nosed realizations in regard to bilateral, economic and security related issues the interactions at the Colloquium recognized that as both countries were deeply committed democracies with shared Asian values, secular and plural polities and truly multicultural societies, it would be mutually beneficial to, inter alia, devote due attention to cultural diplomacy, to strengthening democratic and civil society institutions and building larger and stronger relations within the broader Asia-Pacific framework.

It is hoped that this volume, which contains eleven papers presented at the Colloquium, would be of interest to all those who are involved in contributing towards substantial and sustaining cooperation being established between India and her neighbours.

I thank Prof. Reeves for his continuing help in the organization of the Second Colloquium and towards bringing out this volume, and all the participants for their interest and valuable contributions. I am grateful to the Ministry of External Affairs, Government of India, for its continuing support to the NUS-IIC collaborative programme and for enabling this publication to materialize.

I appreciate the effort put in by Ms. Bela Butalia, Deputy Editor at the Centre, and Manohar Publishers & Distributors, for this volume being brought out timely.

Director
India International Centre
New Delhi
September 2002

N.N. VOHRA

Peter Reeves

The Challenges of an Emerging Asia

Mr. Vohra, distinguished guests, friends, my colleagues and I are delighted to be here in New Delhi at this time, in the beautiful surroundings of the India International Centre, for the 'Second India–Singapore Colloquium'. We remember the first meeting, in August 1999, with great pleasure. This is because that meeting, as a new venture, gave an opportunity for discussion and dialogue and because it made it possible for the Singapore delegates to meet a wide-ranging panel of speakers who brought experience and thoughtfulness to the discussion on matters of mutual interest.

How can we highlight the theme of this Colloquium on 'Emerging Asia: Challenges for Singapore and India'? Such a central theme raises a number of immediate issues. In what sense is the continent, which has been the basis for so much intellectual, cultural and material development over the ages, 'emerging'? There is no doubt that the nations of Asia are coming to play an increasingly wider role in world affairs and world development; and they seem certain to provide, in so many ways, the most significant markers of change for the coming century. It is, in fact, striking how different the world is now from that with which we were familiar in 1999, when we met in the First Colloquium. Moreover, the changes which have taken place—and are still in train as we meet—have been searching challenges for us all. Many of the changes are based on longer and deeper causes, of course, but their appearance in these present times nonetheless increases the seriousness of the situation in which India and Singapore (along with many other nations) find themselves. Our discussions in the next two days will touch on a number of these challenges.

*The above is an extract from the inaugural presentation by Professor Peter Reeves, National University of Singapore, who was Co-Convenor of the 'Second India–Singapore Colloquium'.

The challenges which arise from 'emerging Asia' necessarily have to begin with the questions of security and autonomy which have arisen in the aftermath of '9/11'; not just from the shocking events of that day but also from the nature of the responses and actions which have followed. These, on the one hand, have already brought major changes in the disposition of forces in a number of regional 'theatres'. At the same time, they presage a series of challenges to world order, to world peace, to democratic forms and institutions, and to the autonomy and security of individual nation-states around the world. Very importantly, these challenges affect especially Asia—conceived of in its broadest extent—from 'West Asia' to 'Central Asia' and to 'South and South-East Asia'. The shadow of these events, and the reactions to them, will continue to fall over Asia—and the rest of the world—for a long period to come. We will hear informed discussion on these challenges and shifts, and the re-aligning balances which flow from them, over the next two days.

Quite different in nature, but no less significant are the challenges to the economies of Asia—and specifically the economies of India and Singapore—arising from the processes of globalization about which we spoke in our First Colloquium. If anything those challenges are sharper and have more of a cutting edge now than when we last met. The challenges of the WTO arrangements and the movement towards both regional economic blocs and towards FTAs which were already there in 1999 are continuing; but they continue in an economic climate which was not foretold in 1999. That climatic change has shown starkly that, in a globalized world economy, change in one part of the system affects the whole, often with momentous consequences. This, moreover, brings us back to the challenge which has been ever-present and is as significant today as it was a decade or two ago—the challenge of distributive economic justice in Asia (and, of course, in Africa and Latin America). This is the challenge of poverty and its alleviation, especially in areas where the maintenance of peace and security prove difficult to ensure. This points to the weaknesses which lead to other persistent challenges, for example, to the movement of people as 'illegal migrants', 'asylum seekers', 'economic refugees', which is assuming even greater dimensions and to which the powers of a globalizing world economy—seeking the more open and rapid movement of all factors of production (except, perhaps, people)—seems to have no sure answer. Similarly, although in a very different register, there is the challenge of globalization and the effect on cultural autonomy in the era of satellite TV and the Internet. This is the challenge of global absorption, of what—in an old phrase—was 'coca-cola-ization'.

Clearly there are many such 'challenges'. Each of us will have our own 'spin' (as we have learned to call it) on these matters. Suffice it to say that these, and many other areas of concern, will provide the substance of our discussions over the next two days. We have an array of speakers with knowledge and experience in many fields and they will be able to bring us well-considered and well-balanced analyses of the situation that faces Asia, 'emerging Asia' in general and India and Singapore in particular. We will have an opportunity to hear how some of these challenges are being addressed and the likely outcome of such plans and developments and we will no doubt have the opportunity to discuss the further changes that such outcomes may portend. The value of the Colloquium lies precisely in this process of working through such questions in a spirit of dialogue and mutual interest. We are indeed fortunate to have this opportunity to engage in that dialogue and discussion. For that opportunity we express our appreciation of the work of Mr. Vohra and his staff at the India International Centre and to the generosity of the presenters, from both India and Singapore, who have given their time and their talents to the preparation of the papers before us. We will all be more able to judge the challenges to India and Singapore from the new forces working in 'emerging Asia' as a result of their endeavours and the discussions which will ensue.

Kripa Sridharan

Transcending the Region: Singapore's India Policy

INTRODUCTION

Explaining the course of Singapore–India relations in the post-Cold War period is, in one sense, a pleasant task since interactions between the two countries have been positive and on the upswing. Mutually good and bad bilateral relations tend to resemble the situations that happy and unhappy families find themselves in. Happy bilateral relations are all alike. But the unhappy ones can take different forms and features and can be exasperating for both analysts and practitioners. Ties that bind, therefore, are definitely more pleasant to explore and explain.

In the last ten years, one might say, Singapore's India policy has acquired an autonomy that it lacked before. Aware of India's vast potential following India's decision to liberalize its economy, Singapore has been involved in building a multidimensional bilateral equation with India. In doing so it has transcended its region but not abandoned it, as can be seen from its efforts to strengthen Indian involvement in ASEAN-led initiatives, making sure that India is one of the players in the evolving regional balance. The idea is to intertwine the bilateral, associational and regional strands without letting any one of them overshadow the other.

Any consideration of Singapore's relations with India has to be placed within the broad context of Singapore's foreign policy objectives. The main principles of that policy in the words of the government are as follows:[1]

- As a small state, Singapore has no illusions about the state of our region or the world.
- We need to maintain a credible and deterrent military defence to underpin our foreign policy.

- We must promote and work for good relations with our neighbours in all spheres.
- We are friends with all those who wish to be friends with us.
- We stand by our friends who have stood by us in times of need.
- We fully support and are committed to ASEAN.
- We work to maintain a secure and peaceful environment in and around South-East Asia and in the Asia Pacific region.
- We must work to maintain a free and open multilateral trading system.
- We are ready to trade with any state for mutual benefit and will maintain an open market economy.
- We will support and be active in international organizations such as the UN.

Michael Leifer, the well known South-East Asian scholar, published a remarkable account of Singapore's foreign policy shortly before he died last year.[2] He appropriately termed it the foreign policy of an exceptional state, and exceptional it is, in more ways than one. Its exceptionalism derives from many factors. Though a minuscule state it has made its presence felt in the wider world because of its economic achievement and its vigorous diplomacy. It had an exceptional birth, almost the only state that was asked to leave a federation rather than choosing to do so on its own. Its economic success against all odds has been exceptional too. Singapore is also remarkable in the way in which it pursues its domestic and foreign policy objectives. It articulates these in unambiguous terms and never leaves anybody in doubt about the vulnerabilities it faces. Nothing is taken for granted—its survival, its continued prosperity, stable regional or international environment. It is adroit in adapting to changing situations and in using its diplomatic skills to put across its point of view effectively. Together all these have enabled Singapore to carve a place for itself in the international arena. An amazing achievement for a country of this size which has been applauded for having made the most spectacular leap into the league of developed states within a short span of time.

The organizing principle of its foreign policy is realism but of a tempered sort. While recognizing the centrality of the state and the anarchy of the international system its foreign policy acknowledges that anarchy can be mitigated by institutional cooperation and international regimes which make it possible for creating amity between states, making sure that norms and rules are complied with and defectors are brought in line. This is much like the strain evident in liberal institutionalist thinking. Singapore also embraces the view that force should not be a foreign policy instrument but may be unavoidable as a deterrent. All these are hallmarks of pragmatism and well worth keeping in mind while explaining the republic's external relations.[3]

FOREIGN POLICY REORIENTATION

Although Singapore and India have hit it off rather well in the last few years it would be naive to overlook the fact that matters between them had not always been friction free. The foreign policy behaviour of both states towards one another has undergone marked changes in the last ten years.

An adequate theory which explains foreign policy change is conspicuously absent in international relations. But for that matter neither is foreign policy stability explained all that well. Stable relations between states are valued but that does not tell us why they obtain. One way to conceive of both change and stability is to think in terms of cycles.[4] Relations wax and wane, as they have done between Singapore and India, in response to changes at the international, domestic and individual levels. Foreign policy behaviour of actors change because of new inducements and their accompanying benefits and costs. This much is realized by states and accordingly they make an effort to adapt to new situations.

A partial explanation for change can be found by placing foreign policy redirection along a continuum indicating the magnitude of shift from major adjustment changes, through programme changes, goal changes to orientation changes. According to K.J. Holsti they can be subsumed under foreign policy reorientation and restructuring.[5] The intent of foreign policy makers to restructure policy is called foreign policy reorientation; while foreign policy restructuring denotes that the intent has been followed by actual alteration of the total pattern of a state's external actions and transactions. The distinction between intent to change policies and actual re-patterning is important. Reorientation without restructuring is possible, but restructuring without reorientation is not likely. Foreign policy being an interactive process the quality and rate of reorientation is also dependent on the level of reciprocity (in terms of attitude and actions) shown by the targeted state as much as by the initiating state.

Reorientation in Singapore's policy took place at a time when India was also engaged in that exercise which came to be known as India's 'Look East' policy. Policy reorientations on both sides, while not being radical, were definitely pronounced. It would not be an exaggeration to say that India's need and Singapore's interest fitted together 'like sword and sheath'! The change in behaviour that is now evident is a result of reorientation which, in time to come, could produce a substantial restructuring but that has not yet happened.

PAST RELATIONS

Ties between the two countries had reached a low point in the early 1980s. Admittedly, this was not due to any direct bilateral dispute between them but because of their divergent perceptions and policies regarding regional order, stability and great power intrusions within their regions. While bilateral relations even within that context were kept steady there was a noticeable lack of warmth between the two sides. In international forums they were often ranged on opposite sides over issues of regional order arising out of Vietnam's invasion of Cambodia and the Soviet invasion of Afghanistan. Based on their respective links with the superpowers it was not surprising to see them adopt diametrically opposite positions on these issues. It would not be unrealistic to say that their foreign policy behaviour confirmed the neorealist assumption that the international structure determines the behaviour of the units. To a large extent this did seem so and as long as the structure remained the same there was very little chance for behaviour to alter. But mono-causal explanations tend to be partial. Therefore, apart from the systemic factor one must also seek other reasons at the regional, national and individual levels for the less than cordial relations between Singapore and India.

Following the imperatives of the global distribution of power, the South-East Asian states, or more appropriately, the Association of South-East Asian Nations (ASEAN), at the regional level were engaged in building a regional order that was exclusivist. This was the main reason that led them to stall the process which was initiated earlier to make India a dialogue partner of ASEAN in 1980.[6]

ASEAN states in general and Singapore in particular conducted a vigorous diplomacy condemning the violation of international norms by Vietnam when it invaded Cambodia and helped establish the Heng Samrin regime there. The effort at the time was to highlight the starkly distinct pattern of regional behaviour in a differentiated South-East Asia and garner international support to put pressure on Vietnam to reverse its policies in the Indo-China half of the region. Such depictions made for very poor ties with states like India which entertained a divergent view of Vietnamese regional behaviour and compounded it further by recognizing the Vietnamese-installed regime in Cambodia. This was unforgivable as far as the hard line ASEAN states were concerned. Singapore could barely hide its dismay over India's action. Wherever the Cambodian crisis was discussed Singapore and India found themselves on opposite sides.

If the regional climate precluded any close ties there were no compelling domestic reasons for both countries to seek each other out. Both at the functional and politico-strategic levels there was no mutual dependency that existed or was sought. Their economic priorities were very different and the strategies they adopted to achieve those priorities did not call for any serious interaction. On the strategic front there was no scope for dialogue because of their vastly different threat perceptions and security orientations.

Bilateral relations cannot be fully explained without factoring in the perceptions of decision makers. Given the inflexible position that Singapore adopted over the Cambodian issue as against India's pro-Vietnam policy it was not surprising that India was regarded in less than friendly terms by the Republic's key policy makers. They were of the view that the Vietnamese action in Cambodia was part of the larger plot by Soviet Union-led Communist states to advance global communism and eventually realize their dream of global domination. Indian perception was at variance with this view which did not see any connection between the Soviet invasion of Afghanistan and Vietnam's invasion of Cambodia and did not regard it as forming part of a Soviet grand strategy. This gap in perception was complemented by the generally poor opinion in Singapore of India's management of its economy and its inability to handle the various domestic crises that rocked it periodically. India also got a less than complimentary press in Singapore and its marginal utility to South-East Asia was often implied. On the whole, Singapore's perception of India was negative on most counts.

Given assessments constructing any meaningful mutual relationship was impossible and would have been unproductive. But fortunately, this drift was arrested as a result of a whole host of changes that occurred at the end of the 1980s. After a period of relative neglect, ties between India and Singapore took a visible turn for the better in the aftermath of the Cold War. Much of the impetus came from the structural changes that took place at the systemic level. It is not unusual for bilateral relations to improve when there is a conducive international environment. The end of bipolarity meant that these two states did not have to view mutual relations through the prism of their superpower preferences. A more autonomous policy became feasible once the superpower overhang diminished. Their released energies were thus channelled in the direction of finding a more natural level of interaction.

CHANGES IN THE PATTERN OF BEHAVIOUR

The transforming pattern of superpower relations and the change in the distribution of power with the dissolution of the Soviet Union found an immediate echo at the regional level in South-East Asia. The Cambodian conflict began winding down and normalcy was restored through the intervention of the major powers who could speak with one voice in the UN Security Council. ASEAN states played a supportive role in the peacekeeping efforts in Cambodia and reconciliation with Vietnam began taking shape. Under the circumstances, the stridency that was evident in Singapore's diplomacy on the Indo-China conflict lost its edge. Thus the main divisive issue between Singapore and India began eroding, giving way to a more balanced approach. Lee Kuan Yew's visit to India in March 1988 was evidence enough of impending change. The visit helped in downplaying the distortions that had crept into the relationship in the wake of the Cambodian conflict. Lee pointedly observed that although disagreements over the Cambodian issue were quite pronounced in the past, they would not be a major hindrance anymore.[7] A clearer enunciation of this came from the then Foreign Minister Wong Kan Seng: 'For Singapore, the global changes and the settlement of regional disputes such as Afghanistan and Cambodia has opened up the prospects for a closer relationship with India.'[8]

Domestic level imperatives were no less important in contributing to improvement in ties between Singapore and India. This period witnessed Singapore's inclination to explore the possibility of establishing an external economy which, in comparison to the other newly industrialized Asian economies, was underdeveloped.[9] 'All the pre-conditions for Singapore's participation in an external economy (were) present: labour shortages, and manpower constraints; rapidly increasing costs; more competition from surrounding countries, relocation of labour-intensive industries outside of Singapore; companies, particularly, government-linked companies (GLCs) able and willing to operate abroad; and, a healthy level of foreign reserves.'[10] India was looked upon as a possible partner in meeting some of these needs, particularly in the human resources area. No less important a factor in this transformation was India's decision to liberalize its economy. This provided the much needed opening for Singapore to explore the Indian market and regard India as a potential economic partner. Without this important change in India's policy Singapore would not have been drawn to India.

The other domestic consideration revolved around the strategic shape of the region following the demise of the Cold War and its impact on Singapore's security. Following its time-honoured preference for a balance of power mechanism to ensure the survival of states such as itself, Singapore has supported the presence of several big powers in the region. Prompted by this 'multilateralist logic' it was believed that 'India's regional involvement could serve as a counter to the influence of China'[11] following, among other things, the US withdrawal from the bases in the Philippines. Even though initially it was feared that a waning superpower presence in the region would give rise to an unhealthy rivalry between the three major Asian powers, Japan, China and India, with ominous consequences for South-East Asia, this assessment was subsequently revised and the Indian presence was deemed beneficial. B.G. Yeo, the then Minister for Information and the Arts, during his visit to India categorically stated: 'As India integrates its economy into East Asia, India can also help stabilize the region by counterbalancing the other political heavyweights. Because the fear of China will grow with the growth of the Chinese economy, Japan and ASEAN will always value the strategic presence of India.'[12]

Elite perceptions too should be given their due place in determining a shift in policies. Foreign policy is very much an elite-driven activity in Singapore, as it is perhaps elsewhere. But in the case of Singapore the elite imprint, particularly, its Senior Minister Lee

Kuan Yew's, has been more pronounced. Elite articulations of policies have been consistent both 'longitudinally' (over time) and 'latitudinally' (among key decision-makers).[13] As a result, 'the management of foreign policy has correspondingly never been a complex process'.[14] What was shaped in the initial period of its independence by three men, Lee Kuan Yew, S. Rajaratnam and Toh Chin Chye, has continued to hold and the next generation of leaders have more or less followed the same pattern.[15] This is not surprising since core foreign policy objectives of states tend to remain constant and therefore continuity rather than change happens to be the norm in the foreign policy world. But while talking about objectives we should distinguish between core, middle and short term objectives. While core objectives have a near permanent status the middle and short term objectives do tend to shift. When these are combined with leadership changes there is bound to be a reorientation in priorities.

The leadership change from Lee Kuan Yew to Prime Minster Goh Chok Tong has meant a distinct change in the priority accorded to India. Prime Minister Goh has made several trips to India indicating the seriousness with which the Singapore side has been pursuing the Indian connection. One important element in the way India is being perceived is the recognition of India's strength in the Information Technology (IT) area and its significance for Singapore. During his trip to India in January 2000 Goh adopted a more persuasive stance as opposed to a suggestive or facilitative one to impress upon India the need to make itself more relevant to its neighbouring region. The economic downturn of 1997 caused attention to wane but no sooner were there signs of recovery Singapore's interest resurfaced. Overall, Singapore's India policy has been substantially reconfigured in the last ten years.

This is not to say that relations with India have become the top priority for Singapore. It would be unrealistic to overlook the fact that for Singapore its immediate neighbours and major powers like the US and China constitute the most important circle. Leifer's book on Singapore's foreign policy barely mentions India as opposed to China which gets a wide coverage, as do its key neighbours. Even though this may be regarded as the author's bias but it is still worthwhile noting that India is not all that critical a factor in Singapore's foreign policy calculations.[16] Having said that, in the last ten years a very conscious effort has been made by Singapore to seek out India and among its burgeoning external relations the one with India does stand out. As the President of Singapore S.R. Nathan observed, 'Any outside observer would have noted the forward momentum in our bilateral relations in recent years.'[17]

Singapore's India policy therefore is not a mere posturing as it is convinced of India's vast potential and seeks to deepen bilateral ties across several dimensions. It is also keen to get India engaged in the South-East Asian region by enhancing its formal linkages with ASEAN and by extension, with the evolving security scenario in the larger Asia-Pacific region. During his last trip to India in January 2000 Prime Minister Goh Chok Tong said that the purpose of his visit was to persuade India to look towards South-East Asia, ASEAN and Singapore, thereby indicating the three levels, regional, organizational and bilateral, which India should target more purposefully. India too has broadened its vision and has identified the South-East Asian region as 'one of the focal points of India's foreign policy, strategic concerns and economic interests'.[18] Never one to mince words, Singapore has been quite forthright in expressing its priorities and needs and what it hopes to achieve by pursuing the Indian connection. While being conscious of its immediate neighbourhood Singapore has not hesitated to factor in the wider region, which is perceived to include China, India and Australia, for fruitful linkages.[19] India's inclusion in this bunch, although of more recent vintage, is noteworthy.

Clearly, both Singapore and India have made a very determined effort from the early 1990s to reach out to one another transcending their respective regions. This can be characterized as 'across-domain' interactions as opposed to intra-regional relations which are very much 'within domain' affairs.

THE BILATERAL STRAND

Bilateral relationships are mainly of three types, each with its own characteristics.[20] The three types are: relationships with allies, with friends and with adversaries. While with allies and adversaries the give and take is quite straightforward, it is with friends that the situation tends to be fluid. These are relations between states that are on good terms but lack extensive dealings with one another. As a result, it is often difficult to come away with a great deal because each side has its own particular compulsions which it is unable to overcome in the absence of identical interests. (One must distinguish between compatibility and identity of interests.) Singapore-India relations exhibit this situation to a large extent. That is why, after these many years of close contact, the impact factor seems to be still missing and Prime Minister Goh probably had this in mind when he came calling in January 2000. This is, however, now being addressed in a way since Singapore has widened the areas in which it seeks to work together with India. Relations are beginning to acquire a multi-dimensional aspect. Non-traditional areas of interest, such as in the educational field too, are being actively explored.

A thumbnail sketch of the expanding ties might indicate the seriousness with which India is being perceived as a valuable partner. Singapore has positioned itself as a long-term economic partner of India. Bilateral trade has been showing a consistent increase, averaging 9.6 per cent per annum over the past ten years. The total trade value between Singapore and India for the year 2000 amounted to US $3.7 billion. For the first six months of 2001, total trade was US $2.2 billion, up 10.1 per cent over the same period in 2000.

A major part of this growth emanated from India's booming IT sector. Strong consumer demand for electronics yielded a 269 per cent growth in Singapore's electronics exports to India in 2000. Singapore is now India's top import source of electronics, accounting for 21 per cent of India's total electronics imports.

Investments too have shown a robust increase. Singapore is India's eighth largest investor, with direct equity investments amounting to about US $1.3 billion. In the last five years Singapore's investments in India have increased by five times. India's investment in Singapore has also grown by an average of 14 per cent over the past decade, and more than 300 Indian IT enterprises have set up software development operations in Singapore.

Recently, an India Centre was set up in Singapore which is a physical facility to help Indian companies expand and globalize through the Singapore connection.[21] Temasek Capital has set up an incubator facility in Chennai, called inCube, to help facilitate Indian start-ups and an Indian IT services start-up, eGurkha, has capitalized on the inCube programme to establish a presence in Singapore.

It is hoped that the various economic cooperation initiatives between the two countries will be brought under one umbrella, the Closer Economic Partnership framework. Singapore is very enthusiastic about realizing Prime Minister Goh's Asian Belt of IT cities, drawing its strength by 'pooling together India's software expertise, with Korea's broadband capabilities, Japan's wireless innovations, Malaysia's Multimedia Supercorridor and Singapore's infrastructure capabilities'.[22] On the whole, Singapore seems upbeat about the opportunities that lie ahead even though it is not unaware of the hassles of doing business in India. Yet Singapore has been actively promoting the idea that it could be to India what Hong Kong is to China, serving as a gateway into India and an outpost for Indian businessmen to explore South-East Asia and beyond. Further evidence of this optimism was on display during Prime Minister Vajpayee's visit to Singapore in April 2002 when both sides agreed to set up a study group to promote an Economic Partnership Agreement (EPA) between the two countries. Apart from boosting trade the EPA would include 'customs cooperation, intellectual property and financial sector links'.[23]

Singapore has also been actively sourcing talent from India. Aware of the software skills of Indian professionals Singapore has been openly inviting them to make the island state their second home. Prime Minister Goh openly called for India to lose some of these professionals to Singapore instead of losing them to the Silicon Valley!

Even at the level of higher education and research a remarkable opening towards India is apparent. The National University of Singapore has been trying to foster research collaborations and partnerships in the fields of engineering, IT, physical and life sciences with Indian institutions. The President of NUS acknowledged that Singapore had a great deal to learn from these institutions where infrastructural shortcomings had not prevented research standards from being globally competitive.[24]

Cultural cooperation between the two countries has also registered a significant increase. During President Narayanan's trip to Singapore in November 2000 the Third Executive Programme Document was signed which allows both countries to undertake collaborative exchanges in the fields of art and culture.

Another important area of interaction has been in the defence field. India regularly trains naval personnel from Singapore in anti-submarine warfare. Reportedly, defence scientists from both sides are also working together in a variety of areas including artillery systems. Although this is a very sketchy account of the scale and scope of transactions it nevertheless provides some insight about policy consistency and the reasons for targeting India. More importantly, it confirms that both functional and directional changes in policies have occurred.

THE MULTILATERAL DIMENSION

Sinagpore's approach to India has not been confined to exchanges at the bilateral level. As a core member of ASEAN it has been instrumental in facilitating India's formal linkages with the association and has been relentless in its advocacy of India as a valuable external partner of ASEAN. Even though ASEAN is only a shadow of its former self, in some respects it is still a regional organization that defines South-East Asia. It may very well be a candidate for revitalization which, while attracting partners, seems to suffer from a performance anxiety but is still a useful vehicle with which to engage the region. ASEAN has been reinventing itself by facilitating mega-regionalism thus embracing the principle of open regionalism. As a result, it provides an ideal conduit allowing India to transcend its own region and become a player in the extended Asia-Pacific region. Looking East is made easy this way rather than going it alone. Not surprisingly therefore, India has been very keen to become a part of ASEAN-driven initiatives and has found Singapore a very obliging facilitator in this quest.

Thus Singapore's bilateral and associational impulses are entwined with the equally important objective of championing India's cause in South-East Asia. In the mid-1990s Singapore calculated that India may have its own internal political problems and may not move all that swiftly in the direction of implementing the economic reforms[25] but was equally aware that such a large country with so much potential could not be ignored. It was therefore thought imprudent not to ignore an important power sitting astride a vital sea lane. In addition, there was also a recognition that India had not displayed any expansionist tendencies in the past unlike the other two major Asian powers, namely, China and Japan, and therefore would not pose any threat to the region. If anything, it could very well be a counterweight to the other extra-regional powers. This led Singapore to canvass India's case persuasively with its regional partners, who while not being totally averse to India's inclusion as a 'dialogue partner' were not visibly enamoured of the idea either. Reportedly, Singapore was busy behind the scenes in trying to convince the reluctant ASEAN members of the usefulness of India's formal presence in the association. Not only some regional states but extra-regional powers were also not all that enthusiastic about engaging India in this way but Singapore's arguments about the merits of India's inclusion could not be brushed aside by them.

This type of thinking on Singapore's part combines a curious strain of both realism and liberal institutionalism. There is a balance of power logic in involving as many powers as possible within the region, notwithstanding the 1971 declaratory commitment to the Zone of Peace, Freedom and Neutrality (ZOPFAN). At the same time there is an effort to use the regional organization as a vehicle for discussing economic and political issues through the ASEAN Post Ministerial Conference initiative. As Michael Leifer notes:

> . . . at the fifth meeting of ASEAN's heads of government in Bangkok in December 1995 Prime Minister Goh Chok Tong secured the support of President Suharto in a successful attempt to have India recognized as a 'dialogue partner' of the Association. Singapore's relations with India had developed through economic associations as the island-state began to deploy investment offshore for much the same reasons as multinationals had located there during the late 1960s. Apart from sweetening the investment climate in India by helping to extend the diplomatic profile and standing, Singapore was also moved by its multilateralist logic. This had worked with Indonesia when it was argued that India's regional involvement could serve as a counter to the influence of China, which had also been pressing for dialogue partner status with ASEAN.[26]

The same reasons prompted Singapore to seek a place for India within the ASEAN Regional Forum (ARF). Even though India was made a full dialogue partner this had not automatically ensured a place for it in the ARF. Singapore's efforts in getting India admitted are well recognized by the Indians.

Although still very much committed to ASEAN, Singapore has also been realistic enough to understand the limitations of a post-Cold War and post-regional economic-turmoil ASEAN. The multiple crises of the second half of the 1990s left ASEAN in a much debilitated state. ASEAN's near paralysis at a time when urgent action was needed to tackle the economic, ecological and political turmoil buffeting the region considerably dented its image. Ever since that time and probably even before that members like Singapore were engaged in a critical self-appraisal of the association wondering how it could be rescued from possible redundancy. This is not to say that ASEAN is regarded as a spent force but there is a desire to look beyond regional confines. In this sense, much like Britain's attitude to Europe, Singapore displays an ambivalence. It is in South-East Asia but is it of South-East Asia? This is not always clear. Therefore, the search beyond the ASEAN option to a more enlarged and extended edifice of regional security began exercising the minds of the policy-makers in the wake of the Cold War.

ARF, a form of cooperative security that Singapore was actively engaged in crafting, seemed to offer a better scope to allay the persistent security concerns of the island state and also to keep the association relevant. While being ASEAN-driven, which meant that there was no overt downgrading of the association and therefore not objectionable to the other members, ARF had the advantage of grouping all the important regional and extra-regional actors under one framework and in this sense, answered Singapore's multilateral ideal of engaging all the powers in a regular security dialogue. Leaving India out of such a structure did not seem to make sense to Singapore. It lobbied hard to get the reluctant members of the ARF to see its point of view and eventually succeeded in getting their endorsement for India's participation.

Mega-regionalism of the kind represented by the ASEAN Plus Three (APT) initiative, that includes China, Japan and South Korea, has also become a vehicle for revitalizing the regional organization. India displayed a keenness to become a part of it. Singapore raised the issue of India's participation in ASEAN + 3 Summit in November 2000 but found the other members reluctant to agree to the proposal. Malaysia, Thailand and the Philippines were of the opinion that the APT Summit itself was a new process which needed to be consolidated and therefore it was felt that any expansion would put unnecessary strain on it. Malaysia had also been lukewarm to the idea of ASEAN-India summit on the grounds that engagement as a dialogue partner was sufficient.[27] Once again it was Singapore which managed to obtain the required consensus from the reluctant ASEAN members to win the case for India. Referring to the Summit which is due to be held in November 2002 in

Phnom Penh, in his Singapore Lecture Prime Minister Vajpayee openly acknowledged Singapore's 'energetic espousal of India-ASEAN dialogue'.[28]

RELATED AREAS OF CONVERGENCE

Singapore's reasons for viewing Indian participation in regional arrangements in positive terms has received a boost from the altered way in which India itself has begun entertaining a more balanced approach to power politics and has shown an inclination to deal more realistically with the great powers. Singapore has been openly appreciative of India's efforts to engage with the major powers as opposed to being satisfied with carving a 'big' niche in the politico-strategically insignificant Third World arena. Taking note of the visits that have been paid to New Delhi by leaders of the US, Russia, China and the various European countries and the reciprocal visits from India to these countries, Singapore feels that India has re-emerged as a diplomatic player on the world stage.[29] This assessment, which was made even prior to the events leading to last September's terrorist attacks on the US and the subsequent US-inspired war on global terrorism, has been reinforced further.

As uncertainties mount in the international environment and as they get reflected in regional and national arenas there is going to be a need for states to seek common structures of a stable and predictable order around them. In the Asia-Pacific region, as elsewhere, there is no firm basis on which such an order can rest. Therefore Singapore's preference for a multi-pronged balance of power which includes states like India seems to make sense. India too is inclined to see benefits in such an arrangement whatever may have been its past reservations on this score. It is no longer dismissive of such options and this has created a new confluence of interest between the two countries. India values Singapore as a much needed facilitator and recognizes that the island state has exerted a great deal on its behalf to reintroduce it to the region as a potentially major power of consequence.

Between Singapore and India there now exists a convergence of views on the US presence in the region. There was a time when India fretted about the intended scope and scale of US presence in South-East Asia in the post-Cold War era and was perturbed by

Singapore's decision to provide access and support facilities for the US navy and air force. But now it is more relaxed about the US presence all-around the region including its own and sees it as a stabilizing force.[30] The unprecedented defence cooperation between India and the US has significantly transformed this bilateral relationship. The US perceives the military-to-military cooperation as central to the maintenance of long-term stability in Asia. This must sound reassuring to Singapore. This is not to say that Singapore views American unilateralism in uncritical terms.[31] It fears that it may not win America many friends in the Asia-Pacific region. Indian views on this may be very close to the Singaporean one notwithstanding the burgeoning ties between the US and India.

Similarly, India's equations with China too are of concern to Singapore. There was an uneasiness in Singapore about the way the new Bush administration went about cultivating India in the context of its China policy which, it was felt, would add to regional uncertainties, given the natural rivalry between the two Asian powers. But Singapore has, of late, felt greatly reassured by the way India and China have handled their mutual relations despite their unresolved border problem, Sino-Pakistan relations and Myanmar-China interactions. Beijing's isolation is not a preferred choice for either Singapore or India. They would like to see a China acting more in tune with prevailing international norms. China's 'socialization' rather than marginalization is perceived by both to be more stabilizing in the long run.

In sum, these overlapping areas of mutual concern have proved useful in cementing the ties between Singapore and India. It is said that the causes leading up to an event are more interesting than the event itself (Cicero) and the same may be said of Singapore's India policy. What has been sketched here is a combination of factors that led Singapore to reorient its policy towards India. A great deal of faith has marked this initiative which has so far yielded some benefits. Admittedly, not all of these are tangible, but on that count cannot be dismissed as trivial. A sustained relationship driven by both intrinsic bilateral needs as well as common multilateral interests seems to have taken shape. Singapore's commitment and India's receptivity makes one optimistic about the future of this relationship.

NOTES

1. As stated by Singapore's Ministry of Foreign Affairs. http://www.mfa.gov.sg/policy/index.htm
2. Michael Leifer, *Singapore's Foreign Policy: Coping with Vulnerability*, London: Routledge, 2000.
3. Studies on Singapore's foreign policy include Obaid Ul Haq, 'Foreign Policy' in Jon S.T. Quah, Chan Heng Chee and Seah Chee Meow (eds.), *Government and Politics of Singapore,* Singapore: Oxford University Press, 1985, pp. 276–308; Bilveer Singh, *Singapore: Foreign Policy Imperatives of a Small State,* Singapore: Heinemann, 1988; and N. Ganesan, 'Singapore's Foreign Policy Terrain', *Asian Affairs,* vol. 19(2), Summer 1992, pp. 67–79.
4. Robert Jervis, 'Variation, Change and Transitions in International Politics', *Review of International Studies*, vol. 27 (Special Volume), December 2001, pp. 281–97.
5. K.J. Holsti, *Why Nations Realign; Foreign Policy Restructuring in the Postwar World,* London: George Allen and Unwin, 1982, pp. 2, 12–14.
6. India's formal link with ASEAN has had a long gestation period. And even now it is not very clearly understood by many Indian observers that what was sought by India was not a membership of ASEAN. Neither did ASEAN, at any time, consider India as a potential member. Right from the time of its inception ASEAN was very strictly defined in terms of the geographical region. Only South-East Asian states were on the cards for membership, except for a fleeting moment when Sri Lanka was seen as a possible candidate. For details see Kripa Sridharan, *The ASEAN Region in India's Foreign Policy,* Aldershot, UK: Dartmouth Publishing Co., 1996, pp. 47–50.
7. *The Straits Times,* 17 and 18 March 1988.
8. See *Speeches: A Bi-Monthly Selection of Ministerial Speeches*, Singapore: Ministry of Information and the Arts, vol. 16(2), March–April 1992, p. 30.
9. For details on the impetus for developing an external wing see Arun Mahizhnan, 'Developing Singapore's External Economy', *Southeast Asian Affairs 1994,* Singapore: Institute of Southeast Asian Studies, 1994.
10. G. Shantakumar, 'Human Resources Complementarities Between Singapore and India: Formulating Strategies for a Win-Win Situation', in Yong Mun Cheong and V.V. Bhanoji Rao (eds.), *Singapore-India Relations: A Primer,* Singapore: University of Singapore Press, 1995, p. 247.
11. Leifer, op. cit., p. 137.
12. *Speeches: A Bimonthly Selection of Ministerial Speeches*, Singapore: Ministry of Information and the Arts, vol. 17(1), January–February 1993, p. 23.
13. Robert O. Tilman, 'Singapore's Foreign Policy', mimeo, The Fletcher School, Mass., 1985, pp. 2–3.
14. Leifer, op. cit., p. 6.
15. Ibid.
16. India has also merited only a marginal mention in Bilveer Singh's *The*

Vulnerability of Small States Revisited: A Study of Singapore's Post-Cold War Foreign Policy, Yogyakarta: Gadjah Mada University Press, 1999.

17. Speech by President Nathan at the banquet held in honour of President Narayanan, 10 November 2000, http://app.internet.gov.sg.
18. As stated by Prime Minister Vajpayee during his visit to Singapore. See *The Straits Times,* 10 April 2002.
19. Speech by B.G. (N.S.) George Yeo at the SGH Lecture, 29 April 2001, http://www.gov.sg/singov/
20. Glenn P. Hastedt, *American Foreign Policy: Past, Present and Future,* New Jersey: Prentice Hall, 2000, p. 286.
21. The figures mentioned here have been taken from the speeches by various Singapore Ministers during their visits to India.
22. Speech by Khaw Boon Wan, Senior Minister of State, Ministry of Transport and Ministry of Information and the Arts, 7 December 2001, http://app.internet.gov.sg/data/sprinter/pr/archives/2001.
23. *The Straits Times,* 9 April 2002.
24. Ibid., 2 February 2002.
25. Speech by B.G. (N.S.) George Yeo at the launch of India Centre in Singapore, 12 October 2001, http://www.gov.sg/singov/announce/121001gy.htm.
26. Leifer, op. cit., p. 137.
27. *Hindu-International Edition,* 17 November 2001.
28. *The Straits Times,* 10 April 2002.
29. See Foreign Minister Jayakumar's observations as reported in the *Straits Times,* 11 November 2000.
30. See Jim Hoagland, 'India Looks with New Favour on a Natural Ally', *International Herald Tribune*, 22 January 2002.
31. *The Straits Times* (editorial), 19 February 2002.

S.D. Muni

India and Singapore: Bilateral Issues

INTRODUCTION

India and Singapore have four possible areas of constructive engagement in pursuance of their bilateral relations, namely, political (related to the system), economic, strategic and regional, and cultural.

The political systems of the two countries have two strong common characteristics. Both countries are secular and plural polities. The state in India and Singapore does not accord political predominance to any religion, language or race/ethnicity despite the presence of dominant majorities in the respective societies. Both the states also recognize the principle that rights and identities of the minority social groups have to be respected and protected. This is almost a precondition for internal stability and balance within these countries. There may be deviations from the principles of secular-ism and pluralism in practice in some cases, but such deviations are treated as aberrations to be curbed and disapproved rather than legitimized.

One such aberration currently threatens to creep into bilateral relations. This is concerning Singapore's growing uneasiness at the rise of Islamic sentiments, particularly among the Malay community. Since the latter half of the year 2000 particularly, Singapore's Senior Minister, Lee Kuan Yew, has been carrying out extended discussions with the Malay community on this aspect. Singapore's fear of its plural ethnic balance being disturbed has become more acute after 11 September as the presence of Al-Qaeda links in Singapore since December are being eliminated. The ethnic and religious identity issue of the Muslims (Malays, Indonesians and Indians) in Singapore is impinging on the dress code in schools, specially the headdress for girls. Lee Kuan Yew's admonition that the Muslim community, including Indian Muslims, is not doing enough to curb religious extremism have been rebuffed by the community leaders who hold Singapore's controlled democratic functioning as a cause of ethnic tensions. One hopes that this issue does not impinge on Singapore's relations with its neighbours, including India.

Yet the political systems and institutions of the two countries may be called democracies in divergence, although they do not have much affinity for each other as regards the manner in which their governance is carried out. In India's perception, Singapore's democratic system is democratic more in name and form than in substance, with its rigidly operated dominant party system that has not encouraged or allowed the growth of a healthy opposition. The dominant political perception in Singapore is that the growth of an opposition or the evolution of a viable political alternative may generate too much of politics that may lead to unproductive divergence of human energy and creation of political instability, at the cost of national discipline and economic growth. In a typical characterization of Singapore's political system it is said:

> Beginning in the 1960s, the PAP [People's Action Party] government has depoliticised its citizenry and relied increasingly on economic performance to enhance its own legitimacy. Using the language of meritocracy and a paternalistic governing style, the government has successfully marginalised the political opposition. And by co-opting the civil service, the PAP government has achieved an identity of interests with the bureaucratic elite on which it has increasingly drawn for its pool of parliamentarians. In this regard it would be more accurate to speak of a ruling administration in the Singapore case.[1]

Restraints on the freedoms of expression and association in Singapore are not quite compatible with the Indian experience and practice.[2]

As against this, in Singapore's perception, India is a noisy and chaotic democracy. Lack of discipline, lack of accountability and overall inefficiency in the governance are considered as road blocks to economic productivity and progress. Slowness in bringing criminals and disruptionists to book, tardy processes of justice, institutional structures that delay and deter rather than facilitate quick, correct and effective decisions and the mobilization of political support and action along caste, religious and regional identities are seen as the consequences of unorganized governance. Owing to these divergent and conflicting perceptions, very little interaction has taken place at the level of political institutions and interest groups between the two countries. There is hardly any party-to-party relationship, and not many parliamentary delegations have exchanged visits between the two countries. Singapore's controlled system has on many occasions created difficulties for the migrant Indian workers but such issues have been sorted out diplomatically without any tension being created in the bilateral relations.[3]

Due to social plurality and diversity, both India and Singapore have considerable areas of constructive engagement in the cultural field, more so because a sizeable section of the minority in Singapore has Indian roots. One must also concentrate on two important areas of bilateral engagement, i.e. economic cooperation and strategic understanding.

ECONOMIC COOPERATION

Economic cooperation is the backbone of the bilateral engagement between India and Singapore. When Singapore emerged as an independent nation in 1965, India was in an economic mess. And yet, Singapore looked towards India for economic support, investments and trade and India too was willing to offer whatever assisttance it could, in helping Singapore stabilize and consolidate its newly acquired independent status. Gradually, however, Singapore emerged as a strong economy and a dynamic trading nation. It took considerable initiatives to forge deep and diverse economic links with India. There were critical political considerations of its domestic and external balance in looking towards India, but the strengths of the Indian economy, its huge market, its diversified structure of production and its pool of scientific and technical manpower were of special attraction to a growing economy like that of Singapore. In terms of intensity in India-Singapore economic cooperation, one can identify four phases, i.e. the initial period of Singapore's independence, the latter half of the seventies, the latter half of the eighties and the post-Cold War phase.

During the initial phase, Singapore displayed considerable enthusiasm for a multidimensional relationship with India, but economic cooperation did not really take off. There were constraints on India's economic capabilities, and soon Singapore started developing reservations on India's too close economic and strategic proximity with the then Soviet Union, as it chose to follow a liberal, free economy model of development.[4]

During the second phase, India had started opening its economy to the outside world. Japanese investments in the automobile sector (Maruti-Suzuki) were a clear example of this. India's Minister of Banking Pranab Mukherji and Minister of Industries T.A. Pai visited Singapore in 1976. These visits were reciprocated from the Singapore side. As a result of these high level interactions, Indian joint ventures were established in Singapore in textile, auto-parts and sugar production areas. Singapore also laid emphasis on cooperation in the area of tourism, to attract Indian tourists. India had also initiated moves to enhance its economic and politico-strategic engagement with the wider South-East Asian region. India's request, made in December 1976, for a dialogue partnership with ASEAN (Association of South-East Asian Nations) may be recalled in this respect. Attempts to increase cooperation with Singapore fitted well into this wider regional approach. Though there was a new government in India after July 1977, when Indira Gandhi was voted out of power as a result of her emergency rule imposed in 1975, the policy of cultivating the eastern neighbours economically was continued by the successor government headed by Morarji Desai.

India's then Commerce Minister Mohan Dharia visited Singapore in June 1978. Singapore's strong Prime Minister Lee Kuan Yew also visited India in December 1978 to provide impetus to the gradually building cooperation between the two sides. There was of course an important political agenda to Lee Kuan Yew's visit—to dissuade India from supporting Vietnam's military intervention in Cambodia and recognizing its 'puppet regime' there—but possibilities of economic cooperation were also discussed between the two sides. India's request for a dialogue relationship had almost been granted by ASEAN in May 1980, which would have further encouraged economic cooperation between India and Singapore, but India's decision to ignore the ASEAN sensitivities on Cambodia resulted in a setback to this request.

Yet another impetus to India's economic cooperation with Singapore was provided during the later half of the eighties when Rajiv Gandhi succeeded his mother as India's Prime Minister. He also took steps towards liberalizing the Indian economy and forging its linkages with the South-East Asian neighbours. By then, the controversy over the Cambodian issue had also died down due to the Vietnamese withdrawal from Cambodia and the advances in the international peace process on the Cambodian question. This issue did figure at the high level discussions between the Prime Ministers of the two countries during Lee Kuan Yew's visit to India in March 1988. Lee Kuan Yew also expressed his country's readiness to 'act as a gateway' for Indian goods and services to the South-East Asian region.[5] There were frequent exchanges of industrial and business delegations between the two countries. Indians in Singapore set up a number of joint ventures in the manufacturing and services sectors. This period also saw a sharp increase in Singapore's exports to India, more than 50 per cent of which were re-exports of goods from third countries.[6]

It was the beginning of the 1990s that marked a real breakthrough in India-Singapore economic cooperation. While Singapore's economy was buoyant with its sustained dynamism, India, confused and constrained by its serious economic crisis and loss of foreign policy perspective in the emerging strategic structure of the post-Cold War world, was groping for new initiatives. The dynamic region of South-East Asia, in which Singapore was strategically located both from the security as well as economic points of view, was a promising option, as was articulated in India's 'Look East Policy'. Singapore was equally keen in helping India get closer to the ASEAN region. Reflecting the gradual improvement that was taking place in bilateral relations since the latter half of the 1980s, Lee Kuan Yew's successor, Prime Minister Goh Chok Tong, observed:

> Bilateral relations between Singapore and India have reached a stage best characterized as positive and forward looking. The resolution of issues like Cambodia, which had previously caused some problems in Singapore-India relations, and the restructuring of the Indian economy have brought forth fresh opportunities for the two countries to forge closer relations. Both countries could and should now look ahead to a new chapter in bilateral relations.[7]

The Indian and Singaporean prime ministers met on the sidelines of a meeting of the Non-Aligned in Jakarta in September 1992, where Singapore 'evinced keen interest' in getting skilled personnel from India for projects in third countries, and India was keen to enhance investment and trade relations with Singapore. The two Prime Ministers exchanged state visits in 1994; Prime Minister Goh Chok Tong as a special guest at India's Republic Day celebrations, and Prime Minister P.V. Narasimha Rao to formally launch his famous 'Look East Policy' through the 'Singapore Lecture' in

September. Various high-level ministerial delegations exchanged visits. Goh Chok Tong was now talking of injecting a 'mild India fever' in Singapore and the 'forging of a strategic economic alliance with India'. These efforts produced projects like the Technology Park in Bangalore, the proposal for a Madras corridor for Singapore investments and the Tata-Singapore International Airlines bid in the civil aviation sector of India. Moves were also initiated to increase joint ventures in areas like tourism, civil aviation, telecommunication, real estate, highways, financial services, ports and shipping, warehousing, information exchanges, etc. While the Technology Park in Bangalore stands as a monument to bilateral cooperation, the other two projects did not see the light of day. This was also the period when India pursued the proposal of marketing the technologies produced by the Council of Scientific and Industrial Research (CSIR) through Singapore and regular foreign office level consultations were instituted between the two countries. Singapore organized a first ever conference of the Global Indian Entrepreneurs on 19–21 June 1996. India's then Finance Minister, P. Chidambaram, delivered the keynote address. The purpose of this meeting was to stimulate the non-resident Indians (NRIs) to invest in India, possibly in joint ventures with Singaporean entrepreneurs.[8]

An important aspect of India's interest in Singapore for investment has been the frequent visits from India, not only of the central leadership but also the state chief ministers. For instance, in July 1995, almost back-to-back, the Karnataka Chief Minister H.W. Deve Gowda, and the Bihar Chief Minister Laloo Prasad Yadav, took large business delegations to Singapore. Again in May 1997, Andhra Pradesh's technology-savvy Chief Minister, Chandrababu Naidu, and the Maharashtra Chief Minister, Manohar Joshi, took business delegations to Singapore. Most of the chief ministers belonged to political parties which did not have any share in the ruling party/coalition at the centre. This was a clear indication of the broadening political back-up in India for economic cooperation with Singapore. The results are reflected in Singapore's growing investments in India, an idea of which can be had from Table 1.

Along with investments, the trade between India and Singapore had also registered an impressive growth. Indian exports to Singapore included primary products like fish, fruits and vegetables, precious

TABLE 1: APPROVAL FOR FDI IN INDIA

(in Rs millions)

Year	Total World FDI	Singapore FDI	Singapore FDI as % of the total
1991	5341.1	13.7	0.25
1992	38875.4	602.1	1.54
1993	88593.3	667.4	0.75
1994	141871.9	2655.0	1.87
1995	320717.2	9910.4	3.09
1996	361468.0	3197.7	0.88
1997	548913.5	8619.0	1.57
1998	308135.0	7673.4	2.49
1999	283665.34	8258.94	2.91
Total	2097580.74	41597.64	1.98

Source: Data obtained from Indian High Commission in Singapore.

stones and pearls as well as other manufactures like apparel and yarn, data machines and electrical machinery. Singapore exported (including re-exports) to India items like petroleum products, electronic and telecommunication equipment, electrical machinery, chemicals, plastics and scientific instruments. The trade was generally in favour of Singapore. A list of trade figures between the two countries since 1993 is shown in Table 2.

Singapore played a very important role in helping India engage closely with the ASEAN region. By 1995, India secured the status of a full dialogue partner of ASEAN, causing much heartburn to Pakistan, and it also became a full member of the ASEAN

TABLE 2: INDIA'S TRADE WITH SINGAPORE

(in US $ millions)

Year	India's Exports	India's Imports	Total Trade	Balance of Trade
1993	670.5	952.4	1622.9	-281.9
1994	827.0	1320.5	2147.5	-493.5
1995	932.8	1900.7	2833.5	-967.9
1996	1019.1	2090.7	3109.8	-1071.6
1997	1032.2	2198.3	3230.5	-1166.1
1998	613.5	2468.5	3082.0	-1855.0
1999	736.7	2496.1	3232.8	-1759.4

Source: Data obtained from Indian High Commission in Singapore.

Regional Forum (ARF), which deliberates on regional security issues. Singapore has also been actively promoting India's case for joining the ASEAN Plus Three (APT) (Japan, Korea and China), though without success, because of the stiff opposition from some other ASEAN members. It is due to the joint efforts of India and Singapore and due to the support of many other ASEAN members that the India-ASEAN summit level interaction has been institutionalized. While Singapore stands firmly for India's integration with ASEAN and the wider Asia-Pacific region, and is still keen on enhancing economic cooperation, the 'India fever' of the mid-nineties seemed to have declined in Singapore towards the latter half of the 1990s.

There are two possible reasons for that. One, the regional economic crisis in South-East Asia which started in mid-1997, which has had its second phase since 2001, and the overall global economic crisis. The second phase seems to have affected Singapore more seriously as it is passing through a spell of recession and job cuts on a level not witnessed in recent years. There are fears in some quarters in Singapore that the earlier basis of Singapore's prosperity flowing from easy foreign direct investments (FDI) and a focused state-driven policy making process may no longer be sustainable, particularly in the light of China emerging as a serious competitor for FDI. Accordingly, Singapore may have to develop other sectors like information technology, biotechnology and life sciences, and financial services. For this Singapore may not have an adequate pool of human resources. Moreover the regional economy and ASEAN dynamism are also sliding down complicating Singapore's economic challenge.

Second, some of the prestigious, high visibility and heavy-stake (Rs. 2,020 crores) projects like the Tata-SIA airlines, and the Madras corridor failed to materialize, eroding the excitement and even confidence of Singapore investors in India. A stark indication of this could be seen in the withdrawal of the Singapore component from the Tata-SIA bidding for disinvestment of India's flagship carriers, Indian Airlines and Air India. The explanation, offered at a very high political level, was the investors' skepticism regarding India's labour laws, work ethics and management operations.[9]

Under the shadow of the above identified two factors, a subtle shift seems to be taking place in Singapore's emphasis on investment instead of trade in its relations with India. India has already been sounded for a bilateral free trade arrangement (FTA). This appears to be in line with Singapore's decision to have FTAs with Japan and New Zealand. Negotiations are also underway in this regard with the US, EU and Australia. India's response to have an FTA with Singapore has yet to crystallize, given the initial lack of enthusiasm. Indian industry is perhaps not yet prepared to face an open competition with quality products, with a built-in customer care emphasis, that may come from or through Singapore, if the proposed FTA is accepted.

The foregoing underlines the importance of two factors in shaping the dynamics of cooperative economic engagement between India and Singapore. The first, of course, is economic in nature. As mentioned earlier, it deals on the one hand with Singapore's economic buoyancy and on the other with the degree of India's economic reforms and liberalization. With regard to Indian reforms, the disease of corruption in the Indian system is mentioned frequently. Singaporean entrepreneurs are not used to encountering corruption in their dealings at home, but they have shown considerable resilience and skill in dealing with this phenomenon while investing in or trading with many other developing countries like Myanmar, Vietnam, Laos, Cambodia, Thailand, Philippines, etc. Therefore, it is not that corruption in the Indian system—both at the political and bureaucratic decision-making levels—needs to be condoned; it would be misleading to take corruption as an insurmountable hurdle and a serious deterrent to economic engagement. What bothers Singapore's investors most is administrative indecision and delays, and often, confusion about the exact location of authority.

In addition, there are also structural constraints in the Indian system that dampen the enthusiasm of Singaporean investors. Such constraints relate to labour laws, duty structure, customs and other procedures and regulations, political divergence and conflict between the centre and the state administrations, etc. The pace of reforms in the Indian economy has been rather slow and halting, which may be understandable at the level of leadership, but it slows down the progress of stipulated projects on the ground. In January 1995, while building up the India fever in Singapore, Prime Minister Goh Chok Tong remarked: 'I have read criticism that Prime Minister Rao is not liberalising the economy as fast as it should be. But I think the people who made this criticism do not have a full grasp of the difficulties involved in reforming a big and complex country like India.'[10]

On the Indian side, a perception exists at a certain level that Singapore being a Chinese dominated country, its preference for investment destination is China. This contention is supported by comparative figures of Singapore's investments in China and India over the past ten years. The organization of Global Indian Entrepreneurs conference in 1996, mentioned earlier, was also seen by some in India as a confirmation of the ethnic dimension, though positive, in the destination of Singapore's investments. This, however, is not an objective and tenable contention because investment decisions are mostly made on the basis of complex economic criteria, with the growth and stability of returns being one of the principle factors in this regard.

The second factor shaping the dynamics of India-Singapore economic engagement is political in nature. Scholars have argued that after 1971, growing strategic ties between India and the then Soviet Union drove Singapore away from India. Similarly, India's decision to recognize the pro-Vietnamese Heng Samarin regime in Cambodia in July 1980, and the reports of India building a blue water navy in the late eighties, halted the growing momentum in India-Singapore relations.[11] The Cambodian issue had even vitiated India's engagement with ASEAN when its 'almost approved' status as a dialogue partner was withdrawn. In an ostensibly economic cooperation organization, such a decisive role given to political factors was a bit of an anomaly, but that is what it was. There is a creeping perception in Singapore that Indian foreign policy is more oriented towards the West, and therefore pays scant attention to its Asian neighbours. In his banquet address in India in January 2000, the prime minister of Singapore pleaded with his hosts 'to look towards South-East Asia, ASEAN and Singapore. I know that India places importance on its relations with the U.S. and Europe'.

STRATEGIC UNDERSTANDING

India's security concerns have traditionally not extended to Singapore or South-East Asia, though this situation is gradually changing for the past decade or so. In Indian perception, Singapore has an important strategic location in the South China Sea on the sea lanes of communication passing through Malacca Strait. Its proximity to India's outstretched Indian Ocean Islands of Andamans and Nicobar is well acknowledged. With the rise of Singapore as a dynamic economy and an important trading nation, its role as a window on the global weapons technology market is also recognized in India by defence planners.

For Singapore, India is an important security factor for being distant, as well as a closer power of consequence. India's benign historical engagement with the region as a source of culture and trade is a reassuring one, in contrast to other Asian majors like Japan and China. The memories of imperial Japan's encroachment, occupation and expansion still haunt many in the South-East Asian region and China has had a record of being a source of support to Communist insurgencies that rocked the South-East Asian countries until the end of the 1970s. In fact, the Singapore strong man, Lee Kuan Yew, claims credit for dissuading the Chinese leader Deng Xiao Ping from this course of internal destabilization in the region.[12] Being sandwiched between two large neighbours, Malaysia and Indonesia, which are also ethnically diverse and incompatible with the dominant Chinese community of Singapore, and placed in a region where Japan and China can assume hegemonic roles, Singapore seeks security through regional balance and national defence preparedness.[13]

In both these national and regional requirements, India is seen generally as a security asset rather than a liability. Accordingly, a closer identity with secular and multi-ethnic India is considered helpful in reinforcing internal ethnic balance between the Chinese dominant community and Indian and Malay minorities. Again, India can play a positive role in the regional multi-power balance to contain potential regional hegemones. That is why, while cultivating major extra-regional powers like the US, Australia and European countries, Singapore has also facilitated and welcomed India's closer political and security engagement with the region. There have, however, been phases when Singapore entertained reservations, though short-lived, on India's regional security role in South-East Asia. Two such phases may be recalled. One was in the post-1971 period when India had firmed up its strategic ties and security cooperation with the former Soviet Union in order to deal with the situation leading to and arising out of the emergence of Bangladesh. And the second was during the latter half of the 1980s, when Western media reports about India's naval expansion and assertive projections of power in the Indian Ocean had caused what later proved to be a highly exaggerated and ill-conceived scare.[14] In both these cases, Singapore was highly influenced by Western perceptions due to its own close strategic identification with the anti-Communist, Western bloc. India tried its best to clear these misperceptions. Eventually, the end of the Cold War by the end of the 1980s and the collapse of the Soviet Union by the beginning of the 1990s, set at rest concerns regarding India being an extension of Soviet influence in Asia. Singapore also soon corrected its concerns about India's naval expansion in the region.[15]

Soon after becoming an independent country, Singapore approached India for help in the defence field. In 1965, Singapore's leader, Lee Kuan Yew, sought India's assistance in building his country's army.[16] Singapore's security concerns were focused on the Malay Archipelago, since it is sandwiched between Malaysia and Indonesia, and it also feared China's subversive role through Communist insurgencies.[17] These concerns led Singapore to urge upon India to play the role of a 'guardian' by taking 'active interest in the security, political stability and economic development of the smaller South-East Asian nations'.[18] This was also the time that Lee Kuan Yew was suggesting India go nuclear to balance the situation arising out of China's acquisition of nuclear capabilities after its first test in 1964. India was however shy in getting militarily involved in South-East Asia, partly out of fear of getting identified with either side of the bickering neighbours like Malaysia, Indonesia and Singapore, and partly to avoid being misunderstood in the region as seeking a security role on behalf of the former Soviet Union. Subsequently, as noted earlier, the Indo-Soviet strategic relationship also restrained Singapore from pursuing the idea of defence cooperation with India, due to its own strategic proximity to the US. There were also constraints on India's defence capabilities in the aftermath of its military debacle in 1962 at the hands of the Chinese. Only modest defence ties were maintained between India and Singapore involving training facilities and occasional exchange of visits between professional defence institutions.

The question of defence cooperation between India and Singapore was revived by the beginning of the 1990s. India's Prime Minister Narasimha Rao discussed it with his Singapore counterpart during their meeting in Jakarta, in September 1992.[19] From February 1993, India and Singapore started having regular periodic naval exercises. In March 1996, such exercises also involved anti-submarine warfare tactics. Indian naval ships have also been paying regular goodwill visits to Singapore since the mid-1990s. And the Naval Chiefs of the two countries have also maintained regular contacts with each other. In September 1999, the Vice Chief of the Indian Army, Lt. Gen. Chandra Shekhar, attended the first Pacific Army Chiefs Conference, co-hosted by Singapore and the US in Singapore. India and Singapore have also been attending the Defence Expositions organized by each of them. Singapore has also shown interest in some of the defence technologies developed by India in the field of radars and communications.

Considerable potential for sustained defence cooperation between the two countries exists in the field of training. Singapore being a small country, having a total land area of 660 sq. kms, needs space to train its armed forces. The harnessing of this potential fully would depend upon harmonizing procedural details in this field. A critical area is that of compensation for the space and the facilities provided as well as for injuries and casualties suffered during the training period in India. While Singapore prefers international criteria to be applied in working out such compensation, India has difficulties in accepting such standards. A possibility may also exist for India to provide space for stationing some sectors of Singapore's air force. Singapore's air space is also highly limited and congested, forcing it to scatter its fighter planes to other countries like the US, France and Australia. Singapore has also made arrangements for short-term training with Indonesia, South Africa, Bangladesh, Brunei, New Zealand and Canada.[20] India may also offer such facilities on its eastern island territories through mutual agreement. For this, India will have to develop adequate infrastructure and facilities to cater to the needs of Singapore's military.

Another area of cooperation in the security field that has emerged between India and Singapore in the aftermath of the 11 September events is of fighting terrorism together. Both the countries are concerned on this count and can exchange intelligence, monitor terrorist-related financial transactions and coordinate follow-up actions to track down terrorists and their activities.

PROSPECTS

Notwithstanding temporary difficulties, there is little doubt that India's economic reforms as well as its growth will gain momentum and the revival of the global economy will also bring about a change in Singapore's economic confidence. Both these developments together will stimulate greater economic cooperation between the two countries. Besides cooperation in trade and investments, mutually beneficial engagement in the fields of information technology and human resource development offer considerable promise. More so because the process of India's regional integration with South-East Asia has also received a further impetus with the institution of the India-ASEAN summit.

Enhanced economic cooperation between the two countries is likely to provide encouragement to cooperation in other areas, particularly in defence and cultural exchanges. The altered strategic approach of India and the gradual augmentation of its capabilities may encourage it to play a more active and stabilizing role in South-East Asian security. Within this regional framework, bilateral defence cooperation between India and Singapore may also get a boost.

There are no basic conflicts and contentious issues between India and Singapore. The pace and spread of cooperation between them will be defined by their respective perceptions of mutual benefit. The required political understanding exists between the two countries to adjust such mutual perceptions and initiate practical steps to realize the objectives cherished.

NOTES

1. Narayanan Ganeshan, 'Singapore—Realist cum Trading State', in Muthiah Alagappa (ed.), *Asian Security Practice: Material and Ideational Influences*, Stanford, California, Stanford University Press, 1998, p. 605.
2. Suhas Chakma, 'Poor Governance in Singapore', *The Pioneer* (New Delhi), 15 January 1996.
3. Such cases have come to light periodically. In 1982 about 50 Indian workers overstaying in Singapore were deported and during October 1988 and August 1989, their passports were seized. Media reports highlighted such cases.
4. Kripa Sridharan, 'The Evolution and Growth of India-Singapore Relations', in Yong Mun Cheong and V.V. Bhanaji Rao (eds.), *Singapore–India Relations: A Primer*, Centre for Advanced Studies/Singapore University Press, 1995, pp. 22–6.
5. *The Hindu*, 13 March 1988; *Times of India*, 17 March 1988.
6. Mukul G. Asher and Ramkishen S. Rajan, 'Singapore-India Economic Relations: Exploring Synergies for Mutual Benefit', in *Singapore-India Relations*, op. cit., 1995, pp. 116–94.

7. *The Hindu,* 15 January 1992.
8. Ministry of External Affairs, *Annual Reports* from 1990–1 to 1999–2000, Department of External Publicity, New Delhi.
9. Informal discussions in August 2001, Singapore.
10. *The Hindu,* 3 January 1995.
11. Kripa Sridharan, op. cit.
12. Lee Kuan Yew, *From Third World to the First: The Singapore Story, 1965–2000,* Lee Kuan Yew's Memoirs, vol. II, Singapore Press Holdings, Times Edition, Singapore, 2000.
13. Ganeshan, op. cit.
14. Kripa Sridharan, op. cit., pp. 31–2.
15. Ishtiaq Hossain, 'Singapore–India Relations in the Post-Cold War Period', in *Singapore–India Relations,* op. cit., pp. 48–9.
16. Ishtiaq Hossain, ibid.
17. Ganeshan, op. cit.; also see Muthiah Alagappa, 'The Dynamics of International Security in Southeast Asia: Change and Continuity', *Australian Journal of International Affairs,* 45(1), 1991, pp. 1–37.
18. Kripa Sridharan, op. cit., p. 23.
19. *Annual Report, 1992–3*, Ministry of External Affairs, Department of External Publicity, New Delhi, 1992.
20. *International Herald Tribune,* 17 May 2001, 'Cramped Singapore Military Relies on Space Elsewhere'.

Amit Mitra

Growing India–Singapore Synergies in Economic Cooperation

A discussion on the synergies between India and Singapore fits in a way with issues of strategic importance. There are six main points which should be mentioned regarding the synergy between India and Singapore. The *first* point refers to Information Technology. What is most fascinating is that Singapore—the Economic Development Board (EDB) in particular—has built an IT Park in Bangalore which many may not know about. It is an amazing synergy. We have studied it very carefully. There is obviously very deep synergy there. Singapore has also built an India Centre jointly with my organization, i.e. the Federation of Indian Chambers of Commerce and Industry (FICCI) and others, in the heart of the city, attracting small IT entrepreneurs as incubators. They are only given 500 sq. ft. of space and once they set out then they go on to bigger fields. The subscription to the India Centre has been going up. In fact, we expect India Centre to be fully taken up in the future and will join hands with the EDB in other projects including participation of Indian companies in such projects. I am confident that such endeavours will go a long way in establishing the presence of Indian companies in Singapore.

Another interesting aspect is that Singapore allows Entrepreneurial Visa status—something I have never seen elsewhere—where you get a one-year visa to do a start-up and if you succeed you go on, otherwise you stop. And this is particularly in the area of IT. So my first submission is, there is immense potential between India and Singapore in the Information Technology area with their own IT Park here and India Centre in Singapore. We are not exploring this particular mutually beneficial synergy.

Second, there is yet another area where there are tremendous synergies between India and Singapore—biotechnology. The advancements that India and Singapore have made in this industry will facilitate fruitful tie-ups between our R&D institutions. So far there has not been much progress in biotechnology exchange between our two countries although Indian health care facilities are slowly exploring markets in Asia, for instance the Apollo Hospital Group. There is a vast field of genetic engineering, biotechnology and medical diagnostics where our expertise can combine effectively with Singapore, to create a new hub of knowledge-based industries.

I understand that a new biomedical institute is being set up in Singapore to conduct in-depth research in areas of tissue and stem cell re-engineering. Molecular biologists and experts from all over are forging research alliances with leading institutes in Singapore. With our advancement and lead in specialty chemicals, we should explore new connectivities with Singapore in this vast and growing area. It is true that I see natural links between India and Singapore.

May I recall what Peter Drucker, a keen observer of the profound changes in economy and society, said in his well-acclaimed book *Post Capitalist Society*? He called the rise of the knowledge society 'as great a change in intellectual history as any ever recorded' and went on to say that 'in both West and Asia, knowledge had always been seen as applied to *being*. Almost overnight, it came to be applied to *doing*. It became a source and a utility. Knowledge had always been a private good. Almost overnight it became a public good.'

The issue is, how can India and Singapore jointly seek to benefit from this evolution where knowledge has become the resource? Even China has signed an agreement with Singapore to set up an innovation centre as a global launch pad to promote the technologies of Chinese companies. We need similar initiatives to commercialize our products and Singapore can be our useful partner.

One of the major aspects of Singapore is the Infocom Development Authority (IDA), an organization that focuses on physical facility for Information Technology and particularly entertainment. I will just give you some understanding on this. The amount of broadband that IDA has created is about hundred times that available in India. It may come as a surprise that an Indian company called Pentafour, which is today the world's largest animation company, is uplinking 43 Indian channels simultaneously on this broadband space, a completely unutilized broadband space. FICCI will soon be sending a special delegation along with the prime minister which will only focus on e-Entertainment because they (Singapore) have the physical capability and we have the software. India produces the largest number of films; it has one of the largest film productions in the world—television programmes and all kinds of things—while Singapore has the broadband capacity.

Of course, two Indian companies are presently wiring India with fibre optic lines as well as ISDN and ATM switching. Representatives of both came to me and said, 'Why the hell are you promoting Singapore? Very soon we will have as much broadband space as Singapore.' But the issue is, let us start a synergy, then bring the synergy back to India. So, my second submission is that there is tremendous scope in e-Entertainment and broadband.

Today, we are talking of the world of convergence, a world where information technology and entertainment have produced what is termed the industry of infotainment. This will be a growing area and with recent advances in technology, this is also an area where India and Singapore can strive for win-win partnerships. India has already established its niche in software and is steadily progressing towards building the sophisticated infrastructure that will cater to the needs of infotainment. It is here that Singapore could be the best place in Asia for promoting connectivities with India and as a base for international infotainment, especially for the Asia Pacific market.

The *third* point is the financial power of Singapore. I was surprised to find when I was there that they have a massive financial institution which is completely privately held by the government. It is not listed, so you do not know what its balance sheet is like. And the rumour is that they have invested US $ 110 to 140 billion through this one institution. I tried to do some snooping to see what the proportion of this institution's investment in terms of India and elsewhere is. Well, 80 to 85 per cent of the investment is in the developed world. You may walk into a New York skyscraper and find out that in fact Singapore has major holdings in it.

So, their financial power comes not only from garnering other people's resources but also their own resources and what is interesting is the secretiveness. It is not public. Take the case of Indian institutions like the Industrial Development Bank of India (IDBI), Industrial Finance Corporation of India (IFCI) and Industrial Credit and Investment Corporation of India (ICICI). They are all public.

But Singapore's largest powerhouse is not public. In fact, I met one of the vice-presidents of this powerhouse whom I quizzed for one hour and I could not get much information about the nature of their portfolio. So, what is interesting is power as well as the portfolio.

There is yet another dimension that merits consideration. The financial markets experience continuous change and it is essential that the authorities, with appropriate reform measures, ensure a high degree of integration in the financial markets and develop the financial infrastructure. This is even more significant, given that we have 1997 just behind us. In the Asia Pacific region, Hong Kong and Singapore have so far dominated the financial markets. With Hong Kong's ongoing economic integration with China certain complexities have emerged, although it is argued that Hong Kong will continue to be the important administrative headquarter in the region if one plans to invest in China.

The trend that is fast emerging is the rise of Singapore as an extremely important headquarter of Asia's financial markets in the region, with its superior infrastructure and especially if one plans to invest in Thailand, Indonesia, Malaysia or Japan.

Services such as financial funds management, venture capital, leasing and options require extensive esoteric concentrated skills and it is here that India can be a natural partner of Singapore. On the one hand, Indian companies can look at increasing their listings in the Singapore Stock Exchange and on the other hand our legal and accounting skills can complement Singapore's financial skills. This, in my view, will be a harbinger of the growing economic dynamism of our relationship with Singapore.

The *fourth* point is that there are three powerful organizations which work on infrastructure, namely, the Trade Development Board (TDB), the Infocom Development Authority (IDA) and the Economic Development Board (EDB). We in India have a Special Economic Zone and a new policy, very much in line with China's experience, that is, POSITRA, which holds 10 per cent of equity today, though it has not financially closed yet, and there is the JTC from Singapore. Special Economic Zones are their speciality and we have tremendous synergy.

In ports, Singapore is perhaps the world's best today in terms of movement. We are privatizing the ports in India, and Singapore already has some holdings in our ports. Then there are the airports.

As you know, there is Singapore Airlines, then Singapore Airport with the Tatas—there is massive experience, tremendous possibilities, all unexploited. There are yet other fields such as telecom, shipbuilding, urban development, oil and gas where Singapore has tremendous expertise. Companies such as Kevarner, one of the largest Norwegian shipbuilding and oil services group, has picked Singapore as its Asia Pacific hub. This shows the signi-ficance of Singapore in terms of logistics and its connectivity with other parts of the Asia Pacific. As one of our closest neighbours, the time is opportune for us to strengthen our network and tap a wider customer network through Singapore.

Then there are the Special Economic Zones. Singapore builds Special Economic Zones all over the world including China. Why not India? This is a particular aspect of regional cooperation that is redrawing economic boundaries and creating new economic subregions. The offshore special zone which Singapore developed in Suzhou has emerged as a Singapore-sponsored satellite economy. Singapore and India could definitely enhance such partnerships. In any case, this trend is emerging prominently in Asia where Special Economic Zones are becoming the characteristic form of economic entities and conducive to mutual benefits between partners.

My *fifth* point relates to trade. Not only is Singapore the gateway to ASEAN, it can also be an alternative gateway to China. We have companies which are pushing now to use Singapore's expertise as a gateway into China for trade as well as foreign direct investment negotiations. It is interesting to note that over 40 per cent of Chinese exports to Singapore are re-exported, mostly to South-East Asian countries. The TDB of Singapore is encouraging more Chinese companies to set up operations and use Singapore as a centre for their entrepôt trade.

You would be interested to know that Indian business people also often do not want to go into ASEAN countries except through Singapore. By the way, Indian holdings in this area are unbelievable. The largest palm oil refinery in the world is in Malaysia and who owns it? The Aditya Birla Group. Who owns the largest carbon black company in Thailand? The Aditya Birla Group. There are massive amounts of holdings in Indonesia as well. Who owns the largest textile company in Indonesia? The Indo Rama, an Indian group belonging to the Lohias. So, it is fascinating to note that there is a lot of Indian investment in this area of a very large nature, and Singapore is usually the nodal operational point for all these investors.

Singapore is an international city and I do not think it would be far from the truth to call it the melting pot of Asia. This is a nation where the multinationals and the leading financial institutions have based their regional headquarters. This is a country with a distinctive essence that has developed the process of formal and informal commercial and financial networks. With effect from March this year, banks and other financial institutions in the world will be able to lend Singapore denominated stocks and engage in complex financial transactions like currency swaps more freely. It is expected that this will increase the volume of trading of Singapore dollar instruments and assets and will strengthen Singapore's financial stature in the region, leading to more vibrancy in Singapore's stock market. Indian business can, therefore, find in Singapore an optimal setting for both financial and commercial dealings and expand its networks for a wider Asia Pacific as well as global outreach.

The last point I would like to make is on WTO. Off the record, I would like to quote a conversation that I had with the Commerce Minister of Singapore, a very dynamic young man, very intellectually bright. Singapore was taking a position very much in line with the Western position—the West European, European and American position—on Singapore issues, that is, freeing of investment competition policy, environmental policy, even at one time labour policy.

Singapore played a critically important role in this debate of the WTO as an intermediary between various powerful groups. For example, when I said to the Commerce Minister, 'Look, India will sustain its position against all odds', he asked me, 'Who are the allies?' I said, 'South Africa'. He said, 'Rubbish! I just had a talk with the South African Commerce and Industry Minister and his position is different from yours.' Then I said, 'Malaysia, on WTO.' He pulled out the signed documents of APEC and ASEAN and he said, 'Look, Malaysians have signed on the dotted line. What are you talking about? You read it.' It is very fascinating, I mean, he had interloped, as a small country but a very strong-positioned people, into that process.

Now, I did meet him in Doha and I realized again that he is playing a very important role in intermediating, but in a position similar to that of developed countries, because, after all, they have 25,000 dollars per capita income or more. So, they have many characteristics in line with that of a developed country.

On the WTO issue they are our friends and you would be happy to know that our Commerce Minister and their Commerce Minister have a personal friendship, though their positions are diametrically opposite. But they have a friendship, they have a relationship, they are on talking terms, they are on 'platforming' terms and they have good communication motors on both sides. In other words, they could play an important intermediary role, carrying your perspective, debating those perspectives, in the future.

I cannot conclude without mentioning the growing synergies in the area of education and training. One has been increasingly watching Indian students attending courses in the National University of Singapore and the interest that the Singapore Airlines Scholarship has generated amongst Indian students. This augurs well for a growing partnership in the field of education between us. The facilities already exist in Singapore. Her high standards and the commonality of English language will further enable students to study in Singapore as an alternative to the West. Students from Singapore could also benefit from such tie-ups, especially in the field of software training and other value-added services in India.

I would therefore sum up by noting that this in a way is strategic. India can be a strategic partner in IT, e-Entertainment, broadband, infotainment in particular, and in the financial sector, apart from business partnership. A good relationship is possible. Trade can be a gateway to not only ASEAN but to China and finally to the WTO; in the future, China in particular will be of interest after Hong Kong's absorption into the Chinese matrix.

Sanjaya Baru

India and Asia: The Changing Economic Relationship

Geographically, the Republic of India lies in the belly of Asia. It is a nation of continental dimensions with civilizational attributes. Its western reaches touch Central Asia and its eastern reaches lie close to China in the north-east and the Malacca Straits in the south-east. India's maritime neighbours include the states of the Persian Gulf and the nations of Indo-China.

India is the place of origin of Asia's most widely practised religions, Buddhism and Hinduism, and has for centuries also been home to the world's other two great religions, Islam and Christianity. Christianity came to India directly from West Asia, crossing the Arabian Sea, long before Europeans set foot on the subcontinent. Buddhism travelled via Afghanistan and Central Asia into China and Mongolia, leaving behind historic monuments in Bamiyan and Bokhara, in Samarkand and Sinkiang. Hinduism spread across the Himalaya mountains, the plains below and into peninsular India, from where it set sail into Java, Sumatra, Indonesia and the kingdoms of Indo-China. Hindu temples are found even to this day in Vietnam. Islam went to many parts of South-East Asia from India. India's cultural imprint is visible all over Asia.

While history gives us a clear understanding of India's relationship and role in Asia, this is the age of economics, of per capita income and markets. Evaluated against the score of economic growth, purchasing power and trade openness, India lies in the penumbra of 'newly industrializing Asia'. It is for this reason that 'Asia' for many in the West and the East has come to mean 'East and South-East Asia'. India has, for the worshippers of the market, been priced out of Asia. Having been woken up by Asia, when Japan bombed Pearl Harbour on its Pacific Coast and finding so many Chinese, Japanese and Koreans on its West Coast, the United

States quite understandably began its discovery of Asia from the East. Never mind that Europe, in the form of Christopher Columbus, stumbled upon America in search of India!

GEOGRAPHY

Geography textbooks are quite clear about where India lies. Dudley Stamp, the distinguished Australian geographer, reminds us of what European geographers have suggested for a long time, namely, that the world is divided into seven continents—Europe, North and South America, Asia, Australasia (including the islands of the Pacific), Africa and Antarctica. The geographer's Asia begins near Istanbul and ends near Hokkaido. It stretches across West Asia, Central Asia, Eurasia, the Indian subcontinent ('South Asia' is an Americanism, perhaps invented in the US State Department after the Second World War), through China and 'Indo-China' (mark the concept) all the way to Japan.

The French historian Fernand Braudel refers to the 'Malacca peninsula' (present day Malaysia, Thailand and Singapore) and the islands of Java and Sumatra as the 'centre of gravity of the Far East'.[1] Add to this region Vietnam, Laos and Cambodia and you get what Stamp and many other geographers have for long called 'Indo-China'. Why Indo-China? Therein lies the answer to the question of the Asianness of India. India and China were the dominant civilizational entities of Asia impacting on the culture and life of the people of this region for centuries. Note the origin of the name 'Indonesia' itself. Little wonder then that this region is called Indo-China. It is the heart of Asia, of which China is the expansive chest and India the enormous belly. But the purely geographical basis of India's Asianness is all too evident to anyone who looks at a map.

HISTORY AND POLITICS

To be sure, though, the geographical aspect of India's Asianness is not purely cartographic. It is both geopolitical and geo-economic. History bears witness. Consider again Braudel's reflections:

> The Far East taken as a whole, consisted of three gigantic world-economies: Islam, overlooking the Indian Ocean from the Red Sea and the Persian Gulf, and controlling the endless chain of deserts stretching across Asia from Arabia to China; India, whose influence extended throughout the

Indian Ocean, both east and west of Cape Comorin; and China, at once a great territorial power—striking deep into the heart of Asia—and a maritime force, controlling the seas and countries bordering the Pacific. And so it had been for many hundreds of years.[2]

Braudel notes the depth of India's economic integration with Asia and its central position in the history and politics of the continent thus:

The relationship between these huge areas was the result of a series of pendulum movements of greater or lesser strength, either side of the centrally positioned Indian subcontinent. The swing might benefit first the East then the West, redistributing functions, power and political or economic advance. Through all these vicissitudes however, India maintained her central position: her merchants in Gujerat and on the Malabar or Coromandel coasts prevailed for centuries on end against their many competitors—the Arab traders of the Red Sea, the Persian merchants of the Gulf, or the Chinese merchants familiar with the Indonesian seas.[3]

Having conducted his monumental and comprehensive survey of world capitalism Braudel had no doubt at all in his mind that India was an integral part of the 'super world economy' of Asia. However, Braudel also reminds us that it was with the arrival of the Europeans as a maritime force into the waters of the Indian Ocean that India 'gradually lost control of the "country trade" routes throughout Asia'.[4]

The conquest of India by Europe began a process which disrupted the links between the subcontinent and the rest of Asia. The bountiful subcontinental economy and its prosperous trade were delinked from ancient and long-standing links with West and Central Asia, China and Indo-China and linked to Europe and to the wider British Empire. Where India's Asian links were kept alive it was more to destroy Britain's rivals in Asia rather than strengthen India's links with the mother continent. Consider, for instance, the Opium trade with China. Here India was used as a springboard for the conquest of the China market. For centuries India and China had lived as friendly neighbours. There is no recorded history of conflict between any Indian kingdom and the Empire of China. It is the British who sowed the seeds of conflict between these two great Asian powers. The impact of colonialism on the global economic system and the decline of China and India is most graphically depicted by the data put together by the Organization of Economic

Cooperation and Development (OECD) on the distribution of world income over the past three centuries (Table 1).

Even in the case of Indo-China, historically India's links with this region were benign. Even when Hinduism, Buddhism and later Islam spread to this region the process was largely benign, with rarely any conquest and conflict. However, the colonial control of the 'spice route', the desire to establish entrepôts and commercial monopolies, created relationships of inequity in the region which to this day influence Indo-China's attitudes towards India and Indians in the region.

In sum, India's links with Asia to her east were disrupted for the first time in history by the arrival of the Europeans in the region. Europe pursues much the same policy by its not-so-subtle policy of 'divide and engage' when the European Union creates a forum with ASEAN (Association of South-East Asian Nations) and dubs it an 'Europe-Asia' forum and India is kept out. How can 'Europe' engage 'Asia' without India's participation? Till even half a century ago this would have been unthinkable—in India, in the rest of Asia and in all of Europe.

The most important factor contributing to this disruption in the second half of the twentieth century was the Cold War. A second factor was India's inward-oriented model of industrialization after 1950. Both these changed in 1990–1 with the end of the Cold War and India's adoption of an outward-orientation. Asia to India's east was drawn deeply into the Cold War and India's 'non-aligned' status contributed to a weakening of her political links with Asia to her east. This was not the case to begin with. Indeed, in the 1950s India, under Jawaharlal Nehru's leadership, and Indonesia, under

TABLE 1: DISTRIBUTION OF WORLD INCOME 1700–1995

	1700	1820	1890	1952	1978	1995
China	23.1	32.4	13.2	5.2	5.0	10.9
India	22.6	15.7	11.0	3.8	3.4	4.6
Japan	4.5	3.0	2.5	3.4	7.7	8.4
Europe	23.3	26.6	40.3	29.7	27.9	23.8
US	–	1.8	13.8	21.8	21.8	20.9
Russia	3.2	4.8	6.3	9.3	9.2	2.2

Source: Angus Maddison, *Chinese Economic Performance in the Long Run*, Paris: OECD, 1998.

Sukarno's leadership, actively pursued the idea of a new Asia. The Asian Relations Conference was a part of this attempt to forge a new post-colonial Asian identity. Nehru was obsessed by India's Asian identity and Indo-China's Indian roots. The politics of the Cold War on the one hand and India's own 'inward-looking' model of industrial development weakened India's interface with much of Asia to her east.

ECONOMICS

It is the economic dimension which, in the final analysis, appears to overwhelmingly influence post-war perceptions of India's Asianness. Four distinct factors have shaped this perception. First, after the Second World War the United States established strategic relations with Japan and South Korea and with some South-East Asian nations like Philippines, thereby itself emerging as an Asian strategic power. Since India was not part of this anti-Communist alliance and opted to remain 'non-aligned' in the Cold War, US relations with East and South-East Asia accelerated at a pace which diminished India's profile in North America. Europe's preoccupations with its own post-War reconstruction, its focus on the trans-Atlantic relationship, the impact of the Cold War on West European relations with Asian nations and the process of decolonization together combined to reduce Europe's interest in the Indian subcontinent.

Second, the outward-orientation of South-East Asian economies, their decision to pursue an export-oriented growth strategy and their dependence on Western markets increased the interaction between the ASEAN member nations and the trans-Atlantic economies. Third, the 'new relationship' between China and the United States and the early pursuit of outward-oriented industrial development by China, after 1978, increased the interaction between China and the trans-Atlantic, especially North American, nations.

Finally, India's pursuit of an inward-looking model of import-substituting industrialization reduced its own interaction with the industrial market economies of Western Europe and North America.

It is obvious that the Cold War was an important element influencing the first three factors above, and India's self-imposed isolation was a second element. India's share of world trade was 2.0 per cent in the 1950s and declined to 0.5 per cent by the 1980s. Indeed, as late as in 1975 India and China had similar shares of world trade but by 1995 India had a share of 0.7 per cent of the world trade while China's share was close to 4.0 per cent. Asia to our east witnessed a similar expansion in its share of world trade through the 1980s and 1990s, till the Asian financial crisis in the late 1990s (see Table 2).

India's inward-orientation and the lowly share of its exports in world trade as well as the geopolitical and geo-economic dimensions of the Cold War reduced India's global profile. The 1990s were a turning point. Not only did the Cold War cease to shape Western and Asian attitudes about India, but also our own increased outward-orientation has helped to reduce our marginalization. India's 'new economic policies' of the 1990s, emphasizing greater trade and investment liberalization and the high-profile migration of skilled Indian workers and professionals to the West, especially North America, has helped increase India's economic and cultural profile abroad. In short, India's increased globalization is shaping Western perceptions about her once again.

Another factor that has contributed to this new understanding of India's role in the world is the emergence of China as a strategic competitor to the West. China's impressive economic performance in the 1990s and the momentum its economy has gained has woken up the West to the possibility of a new 'superpower' taking shape in Asia. China has begun to impact on the politics and economics of almost all its neighbours, spread across the length and breadth of the Asian landmass. From Iran, Pakistan and Central Asia to the west, Russia and Mongolia in the north-west, to the countries of ASEAN in the south and Japan and Korea in the east, China is today a major strategic and economic player and there is in North America and East Asia increasing interest in the geopolitical and geo-economic implications of China's relentless pursuit of economic growth and its rising military profile.

If the trans-Atlantic nations persist with their myopic post-War and Cold War view of Asia, then it would seem that the whole of Asia has been already linked to the growth engine of the Chinese economy and has come under the shadow of China's power and influence. Perhaps for this reason there is now a willingness to recognize that Asia is larger than China and its southern and eastern neighbours. That Asia includes another nation of a billion people, a nation that has lived as an equal with China for at least three thousand years of recorded history. India and China have

TABLE 2: MACROECONOMIC TRENDS IN THE INDIAN ECONOMY

	1980–1 to 1991–2	1992–3 to 2000–1	1993–4	1994–5	1995–6	1996–7	1997–8	1998–9	1999–2000	2000–1
Agriculture	3.9	3.3	4.1	5.0	-0.9	9.6	-2.4	7.1	0.7	0.9
Industry	6.3	6.5	5.2	10.2	11.6	7.1	4.3	3.4	6.4	6.6
Services	6.4	8.2	7.6	7.1	10.5	7.2	9.8	8.2	9.6	8.3
Total GDP	5.4	6.4	5.9	7.3	7.3	7.8	4.8	6.6	6.4	6.0

Source: *Economic Survey, 2001–1*, Ministry of Finance, Government of India.

been civilizational entities and peaceful neighbours through all of recorded history. Buddhism travelled to China from India and Maoism and Dengism have travelled from China to India. Today China stands as a self-confident power, almost a superpower, but through all of history we were equals. We were Asian, we were civilizationally Asian.

India has always been an Asian country but is once again rediscovering her Asianness. In 1992 the government of Prime Minister P.V. Narasimha Rao launched a policy of greater economic and political engagement with East and South-East Asia, which was dubbed the 'Look East Policy'. This has unleashed renewed interest in India's historical and civilizational links with Asia, but it has also helped promote greater economic relations today. The economic links with ASEAN, Japan and Korea have been on the ascendant. India's trade with Asia has grown faster than its trade with the rest of the world over the past decade. Korea emerged as the fastest growing source of foreign direct investment into India in the late-1990s. Regrettably, though, there has not been a similar growth in Japan's profile in India. Korea has in fact overtaken Japan as a source of foreign direct investment in India. Perhaps, Japan's critical view of India's nuclear tests in 1998 and the imposition of economic sanctions may have played a role. Equally, the persistent slow-down of the Japanese economy and Japan's greater interest in China and South-East Asia has also contributed to the lowered profile of Japan in India. It is with the United States and with South-East Asia that India is increasingly interacting.

EMERGENT INDIA IN A CHANGING ASIA

The past is, however, no basis to judge the future. While the twentieth century has witnessed a dramatic change in the structure and role of Asia in world affairs, the twenty-first century is likely to be even more significant. China is fast emerging as a major global, economic and military power. Industrial capitalism and high-tech industries have taken root in such traditional societies as Japan, Korea, Indo-China and India. On the other hand, West Asia and Central Asia remain economically backward, militarily weak and socially contentious. How the interaction between such diverse societies and economies is going to impact on the region is not yet clear.

Equally, it is not clear how the relations between China, Japan, India, ASEAN and Islamic Asia are going to evolve. From India's perspective, its destiny and future role is critically dependent on sustained economic growth and development. India must be able to increase its share of world income and trade. If India can maintain an average rate of economic growth of 7.0 per cent or above over the next decade, its position will undoubtedly alter. Like China it will be viewed as a 'rising power' with global influence. On the other hand, if India's growth remains constrained at 5.5 per cent then India will be an important Asian nation but with limited global influence. If, however, India were to slide back to the 3.5 per cent–4.0 per cent rate of growth recorded in the period 1950 to 1980, then India would remain pre-occupied with internal problems and challenges and hardly have an important global or Asian profile.[5]

Apart from national income growth, India must also focus on increasing its share of world trade. Till the 1970s, India and China had almost the same share of world trade. In the 1950s India's share was in fact higher than China's at 2.0 per cent but by the 1970s both India and China had a little below 1.0 per cent share of world trade. By the early 1990s, India's share was down to 0.5 per cent while that of China had doubled to over 2.0 per cent. In 2000, China reported a 4.0 per cent share of world trade, while India improved its share to just 0.8 per cent.

India's recent growth acceleration compares favourably with its historical record. In the first half of the twentieth century, from 1890 to 1940, the territories of British India recorded less than 1.0 per cent growth of national income. This is an average of high growth, close to 5.0 per cent, in regions such as the Punjab, the Bombay Presidency and the Madras Presidency. In central and north-eastern India growth was negative, largely on account of the collapse of the agrarian economy. However, after independence the growth rate of GDP was 3.5 per cent in 1950–80, and 5.5 per cent in 1980–90 and over 6.0 per cent in 1992–2001. During this entire post-Independence period, however, India's share of world trade went down from 2.0 per cent in the 1950s to 0.5 per cent by end-1980s. At the turn of the century it was marginally up at around 0.6 per cent. Clearly, India has a long way to go in acquiring a share of world trade commensurate with her economic size and sophistication.

The inward orientation of the Indian economy during the period 1950–90 not only contributed to the reduced share of world trade, but also, more adversely, protected Indian industry from the forces of competition. An insulated, relatively high-cost domestic industrial economy therefore came into being. It is important to recall that India's relative isolation from the world economy was made possible by a variety of economic and political factors. To be sure, the most important factor was the level of satisfaction of domestic enterprise with a restricted access to a limited market. Unlike in the smaller east and south-east economies which were forced to seek external markets because of the small size of their domestic market, Indian industry was content in catering to a large home market and did not look beyond.

In the pre-1990 period, foreign trade was essentially a residual economic activity and trade policy was driven by the need to balance external payment requirements with foreign exchange earned through exports and inward remittances of forex earned by Indians resident abroad. Thus, the three major factors driving export policy were: first, the pressure of external debt servicing; two, the burden of financing food grain and oil imports; three, the obligation to pay for technology imports and royalty on foreign investment. Exports were driven by these payment obligations and, therefore, had to be encouraged through subsidies and incentives.

This was much the same strategy that the inward-oriented Soviet Union and China pursued in the post-War period. However, in 1978 China switched gears and moved on to a different strategy of growth based on increased exposure to external trade and investment flows. Consequently, while India's share of world trade had declined and stagnated, China's share of world trade more than doubled in the same period. China's share of world exports increased from 0.9 per cent in 1980 to as high as 3.3 per cent in 1997.

The differential in the level of integration with the rest of the world was even greater in the case of capital flows. According to the *World Investment Report* China attracted average annual FDI inflows of about US $8.85 billion in the period 1988–93 compared to India's share of $234 million. By 1999, China was attracting over $40 billion in FDI compared to a sum of $2.0 to $3.0 billion in India's case (see Table 3). By comparison with a large continental economy at a similar level of development, like China, India's integration with the world economy is limited. The only area in

TABLE 3: GLOBAL FDI FLOWS

(in US $ millions)

	1988–93	1999
India	234 (0.12%)	2,168 (0.25%)
China	8,852 (4.6%)	40,400 (4.7%)
World	1,90,629	8,65,487
Developing Countries	46,919	2,07,619

Source: *World Investment Report*, UNCTAD, 2000.

which India's exposure to the outside world is larger than China's is in the case of portfolio investment, given the greater openness to foreign investment of the Indian stock market.

It is against this background that the Indian economy has been gradually moving, from being inward-oriented to becoming outward-oriented. The increased openness of the economy, it is hoped, will make domestic enterprise globally competitive and speed up the modernization of the economy. It is also hoped that this process will encourage Indian producers to access the world market and enable development of skills to world standards. The strategic policy thinking that underlies this shift is based on the realization that external economic relations create relations of economic interdependence that contribute to a more stable global economic and political order.[6]

It is clear now that the principal architects of India's 'new economic policies' of the early 1990s had an appreciation of the external political context within which external economic liberalization was pursued. This external factor was the end of the Cold War and the dominant influence of the United States. India had resisted US pressures to liberalize her trade and investment policies till the early 1990s. India joined Brazil and several other developing economies to block progress on further trade liberalization through the Uruguay Round of trade negotiations in GATT.

However, India was forced to change its stance in 1991 because it realized that 'economic engagement', especially with the US, was the new post-Cold War paradigm of international economic relations within which developing countries had to operate. While India's economic policies in the 1990s were publicly never so articulated or defended, the fact remains that the altered external political environment had an important role in shaping India's economic policies in the 1990s.

The Chinese model of external economic liberalization in the 1990s drew India's attention to the foreign policy and external security potential of increased FDI flows. China utilized its open FDI policy to secure for itself a constituency of support within the United States. What the Chinese did was not new. Indeed, most of East and South-East Asia pursued this policy during the Cold War period to ensure a 'balance of power' in the region between China, USSR, United States and subsequently Japan. China neutralized US hostility by opening up its economy to American multinationals. India was slow in adapting to this changed environment, but when it did, the opening of the Indian economy to external trade and investment flows in the 1990s can be viewed as a 'strategic' response to a new, potentially more hostile, external political environment.

While recognizing the strategic importance of greater external trade and investment liberalization, the policy makers were equally alive to the critical importance of reducing external debt exposure. Indeed, the policy, the trade and investment liberalization was in part aimed at shifting the burden of external financing away from debt flows to trade and investment flows. Consequently, after 1991 India pursued a systematic policy of reducing its external debt exposure, particularly in the case of short-term debt, and improving its debt service ratio.

An important element of government policy since 1991 has been to reduce tariffs. Prior to 1991 India had some tariff rates around 300 per cent. The maximum tariff rate was brought down to 45 per cent in 1997–8 and recently to 35 per cent. The government has declared its intention to bring this down further to 20 per cent by 2005. The average trade-weighted tariff rate was estimated to be around 30 per cent, with the highest rates in the case of consumer goods and lower rates for agricultural and capital goods. Apart from reducing tariffs the government has also reduced quantitative restrictions (QRs) on imports and by April 2001 all QRs are slated to go.

Apart from trade liberalization the government has also liberalized foreign currency transactions on the current and capital accounts. While current account transactions have been fully liberalized, the capital account has been gradually liberalized, encouraging Indian professionals and corporates to increase their transactions with the rest of the world. India has always been open to foreign investment but foreign-owned enterprises were highly regulated. Foreign companies are now treated on a par with domestic enterprise and India has entered into bilateral investment protection agreements with many capital-exporting countries. India offers full post-establishment national treatment to foreign enterprises.

Going beyond FDI, the capital market has also been opened up to foreign institutional and portfolio investors. Foreign investors are allowed to buy into stocks and mutual funds and Indian companies have been permitted to list on stock markets abroad, including NYSE and NASDAQ. The external commercial borrowing limits for Indian companies have been eased, after the highly restrictive regime was put in place at the time of the balance of payments crisis in 1990–1, and Indian companies have been permitted to raise funds through global depository receipts (GDRs) and American depository receipts (ADRs).

Within a span of a decade, the Indian economy's integration into the world economy has considerably increased. Only a few minimal restrictions still apply to economic transactions with the outside world, particularly with respect to capital account transactions of Indian nationals. Many of these policy initiatives have been undertaken unilaterally, but some had to be implemented as part of India's policy commitments to the International Monetary Fund (IMF) when India was under a Fund adjustment programme in 1991–3 and as part of India's obligations to the World Trade Organization (WTO) as a signatory of the Marrakesh Declaration.

The critics of the policy of external liberalization have been concerned both about the growth implications of trade openness, particularly the danger of domestic de-industrialization, as well as the impact of foreign capital on indigenous enterprise. Clearly the Indian economy is still passing through a phase of transition and it is too early to hazard a guess on the long-term impact of external liberalization on manufacturing growth and domestic enterprise. The experience of the decade 1991–2001 has so far been mixed.

The overall national income growth accelerated from an average of 5.4 per cent between 1980–1/1991–2 to 6.4 per cent between 1992–3/2000–1. In 1994-7, GDP growth hit a record annual average of 7.5 per cent. Manufacturing growth was as high as 12.0 per cent and 14.9 per cent respectively in 1994–5 and 1995–6, with the average rate of growth for the period 1992–3 to 2000–1 being 7.4 per cent. Decadal averages do not, however, tell the full story.

The first five years, 1992–7, did undoubtedly see an acceleration of growth compared to the five years before the 1991 crisis. However, the second half of the 1990s experienced a slow-down in GDP growth, mainly on account of a deceleration in industrial growth. If India succeeds in sustaining high growth and can become globally more competitive, it can emerge as Asia's second largest economy. However, given the domestic challenge of providing a decent livelihood for more than a billion people, India will remain preoccupied with internal economic development. Hence, it will be committed to national, regional, global, political and economic stability and to good relations with all countries. India's premier goal is national economic development and the assurance of the well-being of its citizens. India's national security will be built on the foundations of economic development and not on military strength. India's nuclear posture also, for this reason, is based on a minimum credible deterrent and a commitment to no-first-use.

TOWARDS A MULTIPOLAR WORLD

The economic rebirth of China and India, the expected resurgence of Japan after the current prolonged slow-down, and the continued development of Korea (perhaps a unified Korea) and of some South-East Asian nations will alter the structure of economic and political power in the twenty-first century not just in Asia but globally. Already over the past half a century the process of growth in Asia has increased the profile of Asian economies. This must reflect itself both in the distribution of power and the management of the world economic and political system. The restructuring of the IMF and World Bank, to better reflect the economic size of Asian nations, the democratization of the WTO, to better cater to the developmental aspirations of Asian peoples, and the expansion of the Security Council, to make it more representative of all societies, religious and ethnic groups and economic and military powers, will be increasingly felt in the years to come. There are moves afoot to create institutions at the Asian level, like the Asian Monetary Fund; there are extra-Asian institutions with an Asian focus like APEC and ASEAN Regional Forum; and there are sub-Asian forums like ASEAN + 3 and ASEAN + 1. All these initiatives will enhance Asia's role in world affairs.

The twenty-first century will see the emergence of a multipolar global system in which the United States, European Union, China, Russia, Japan, ASEAN and India will emerge as key elements in the world economic and political system. International institutions like the UN Security Council, IMF, World Bank, WTO and so on must reflect in their composition and approach the increased profile of Asia. Global peace and stability can only be ensured when global institutions reflect the multipolar nature of the emerging world order.

NOTES

1. Fernand Braudel, *Civilisation and Capitalism, 15th–18th Century*, 3 vols; *The Perspective of the World,* vol. 3, tr. by Sian Reynolds from French, University of California Press, 1992.
2. Ibid., p. 523.
3. Ibid.
4. Ibid., p. 522.
5. For an elaboration of this idea of the strategic implications of alternative growth scenarios for India's role in Asia, see Ashley Tellis, 'South Asia', in *Strategic Asia 2001–2002*, National Bureau of Asian Research, US, 2001.
6. See Sanjaya Baru, 'National Security in an Open Economy,' Public Policy Paper, New Delhi: Indian Council for Research on International Economic Relations (ICRIER), 1999. Available on ICRIER website at www.icrier.res.in

Faizal bin Yahya

India–Singapore Trade Relations: Beyond IT

RESPONDING TO GLOBALIZATION

One of the challenges of globalization[1] is the ongoing effort by the World Trade Organization to set in motion a new round of talks to ensure the survival of the multilateral trading system. From the point of view of economic globalization, this trend has manifested itself through increasing integration among national economies, resulting in the diminishing importance of national boundaries. This trend has been fuelled by national policies aimed at the liberalization of trade and investment and the increasing visibility of trans-boundary issues. This concept of economic globalization runs counter to more protectionist interests that support the concept of economic nationalism, which has manifested itself as resistance to economic reforms. Economic globalization and economic nationalism are the two fundamental forces that are influencing and changing the landscape of the international economy.[2] As national economies succumb to the forces of economic globalization, diverse economies like India and Singapore have had to reassess their economic strategies.

Singapore is supportive of the idea of a multilateral trading system and is itself an open economy. India and a number of developing countries have been critical of the WTO and had rejected calls for a new round of multilateral trade talks before finally agreeing to meet at Doha, the capital of Qatar, in November 2000. Singapore's Prime Minister Goh Chok Tong had urged India not to resist the forces of globalization but to continue to open up its economy.[3] Prime Minister Goh felt that the alternative to a multilateral trading system would be the proliferation of regional trading blocs, such as the North American Free Trade Area (NAFTA), which would exclude other economies.[4]

Although supportive of the WTO's efforts, Singapore is also concluding a range of bilateral Free Trade Agreements (FTAs) with like-minded countries that are favourable to an open trading regime. Singapore believes that bilateral FTAs is one way whereby the idea of free trade could be promoted. Arguably, in the early 1990s Singapore's regionalization policy, aimed at creating an external economic wing for itself, had already identified its limitations and seen the need to create synergies with emerging economies in the Asian region such as India to mutually expand economic development. The need to continue the process of strengthening and diversifying its external economic sector to incorporate a global dimension has been acknowledged by the committee on Singapore's competitiveness. The committee is also of the view that Singapore's external economy should complement its domestic economy by trying to overcome the shortage of domestic resources, a limited market and manpower constraints. On India's part, renewed emphasis on its 'Look East' policy is as much a response to refocusing ties with the South-East Asian region as well as acknowledging that economically, relations with fellow SAARC[5] members are not progressing at a satisfactory pace to meet the demands of its growing population. Unlike the economic diversity and economic cooperation which is found in the economies of South-East Asia, the South Asian region has to contend with serious problems of security and ongoing conflicts which impede economic cooperation between states.

REDISCOVERING THE EAST

While India has to contend with security and regional conflicts in its own backyard, especially since 11 September 2001, this has not stopped India from giving renewed impetus to its 'Look East' policy. If relations with its neighbours in the West are tense and volatile, some diplomatic comfort has resulted from its focus on looking East towards South-East Asia to rediscover old ties. Unable to spur economic cooperation with its neighbours in the South Asian region, India has found alternative willing partners in the South-East Asian region to enhance economic linkages. In this regard, from an economic viewpoint, Singapore is high on India's economic agenda,[6] which begs the question, why would a tiny city-state like Singapore be of significance to an emerging Asian giant like India?

Apart from historical and cultural linkages between India and Singapore, Singapore had been instrumental in creating a niche for India as a Dialogue Partner in the previously inaccessible bloc of South-East Asian states called ASEAN.[7] India's status as a Dialogue Partner allows India to be present at the annual ASEAN meeting and to expand ties with the region.[8] Prime Minister Goh Chok Tong had seen the potential for economic growth between India and the South-East Asian region. In particular, there seems to be an obvious synergy of respective capacities and strengths between both India and Singapore.[9] However, bilateral relations have not been smooth sailing; for example, despite running one of the world's best airlines—Singapore Airlines (SIA)—with the Tata group of companies as its partner, it had failed in its bid to acquire Air India and Indian Airlines. Also, another proposal by both companies to manage an airport in south India had unfortunately run foul of bureaucratic impediments to economic liberalization.[10]

Although economic relations between India and Singapore have hit some rough patches, there has been notable success, especially in the thrust area of Information Technology (IT), that has manifested itself in the development of the Bangalore IT Park.[11] Singapore is keen to forge closer economic relations with India, particularly in the field of IT. Prime Minister Goh is keen to tap on the large Indian manpower pool of IT workers for Singapore.[12] Singapore and India have established a joint task force on IT in early 2000 as well as signing an agreement on economic cooperation in November 2000.[13] The success of the Bangalore IT Park and Mumbai's Gateway Distripark has also enhanced Singapore's brand image in India.[14]

IT LINKAGES

The Bangalore IT Park often comes to mind when talk of India-Singapore economic cooperation comes to mind. Built at a cost of US $600 million (S $1.1 billion), the Bangalore IT Park symbolizes the potential for increased bilateral economic linkages between the two countries. Phase one of the IT Park has been fully occupied by 91 companies including some familiar foreign multinational corporations like Hitachi, Sanyo, Glaxo, Tata, GE Plastics, Siemens and Sharp (*The Straits Times*, Singapore, 30 November 2000). Construction of phase two of the IT Park is nearing completion and when completed it will deliver an additional 650,000 sq. ft. of office space. Some S$ 62 million have been pumped into the construction of phase two of the IT Park (*The Straits Times*, ibid.). According to Singapore's Trade and Industry Minister George Yeo, the Bangalore IT Park has become an important icon of the bilateral relationship between India and Singapore (ibid.).

The IT sector represents a very important component of Singapore's bilateral trade with India. As shown in Table 1 the trade levels between both countries have been maintained around the S$ 1700 million mark from the end of 2000 to the third quarter of 2001.

India is Singapore's fifteenth largest trading partner and is set to become a key economic partner in the foreseeable future.[15] According to the Singapore Ministry of Trade and Industry three key factors would boost the economic ties between both countries. These are: (a) India's insatiable demand for electronic goods, (b) India's large pool of IT professionals, and (c) the attractiveness of Singapore's infrastructure and connections to the South-East Asian region as well as to international markets. In the year 2000, Singapore's exports to India were around the S$ 4.8 billion mark, while imports were approximately S $1.9 billion. By the end of 2001, Singapore had become India's top source for electronic goods, accounting for 21 per cent of India's total electronic imports. This places Singapore ahead of the United States which provided 17 per cent, with the European Union (EU) coming third, accounting for 15 per cent of India's total electronic imports.[16]

TABLE 1: SINGAPORE–INDIA BILATERAL TRADE COMPARISON, END 2000 TO 2001

Quarter	Exports S $ Million	Imports S $ Million	Total Trade S $ Million
Q4–2000	1199	558	1757
Q1–2001	1251	536	1787
Q2–2001	1207	486	1693
Q3–2001	1250	444	1694

Source: *India News*, High Commission of India, Singapore, vol. 10, no. 3. November 2001.

SINGAPORE'S INVESTMENTS

Although Singapore's total direct investment overseas is still in its infancy stage, the deregulation of the Indian economy and the process of regionalization by the Singapore government have seen Singapore steadily increasing its direct investments in India. In 1999, it was estimated that Singapore's direct investments in India had reached the $350 million. While the bulk of Singapore's investments have been in the financial, commerce and manufacturing sectors, emerging sectors such as telecom are bond to further increase the share of Singapore investments in India.[17]

Venture capitalists including those from Singapore are also making a beeline for Indian shores. Rough estimates puts the venture capital (VC) funds flowing into India at more than US $1 billion in 2001, an increase from US $750 million in 2000 and only US $20 million in 1996.[18] India has been courted by VC capitalists because of the potential wealth that Indian entrepreneurs can create. Among Forbes' list of 400 richest Americans, seven are Indian immigrants.[19] The Singapore government has allocated US $1 billion in 1999 to form a Technopreneur Investment Fund (TIF). The specific aim is to turn Singapore into the venture capital for the Asia Pacific[20] by not only drawing venture capital firms to Singapore but also by investing venture capital in regional economies like India.

The manager of the TIF, Singapore's National Science and Technology Board (NSTB), has established partnerships with some of the world's largest and most active venture capitalists. The NSTB expects US $1.4 billion to be managed out of Singapore and believes that the multiplier effect of the seed money will be threefold. From the US $1 billion start-up fund, NSTB has allocated US $250 million to form strategic alliances; another US $250 million is to fund companies in their infancy stage of development and a further US $500 million is to be used for broad-based investments.[21]

Apart from the NSTB route, the Singapore government is also taking a direct lead on venture capitalism in India by directing its investment arm, Temasek Holdings,[22] to launch an incubation programme in India for technology companies. The programme, named inCube India, provides an integrated approach to supporting and adding value to start-ups and infant-stage technology companies to accelerate their growth and entry in the global market.[23] The approach taken by inCube would be to use Temasek's range of contacts with companies worldwide to provide incubation companies with access to professional services such as legal and management support resources through Temasek's affinity partners.[24]

The Managing Director of inCube, Wong Lin Hong, said that 'India is known for strong technology and software skills'. Chennai in southern India was chosen to launch the inCube programme in India. The 8,600 sq. ft. incubation centre will be used initially as a window for Temasek to network and select Indian companies for its incubation programme.[25] Adopting a cluster strategy to maximize the benefits of synergies, incubating companies with related and complimentary products and services would be grouped and housed together to enable them to take advantage of each other's expertise and provide well rounded solutions to various problems. InCube India will be focusing on technology start-ups in the following areas:

- Internet Enabling Software/Product
- Wireless Communications
- Applications Service Providers (ASPs)
- Telecommunications
- Artificial Intelligence
- Embedded Software

INDIA CENTRE

Bilateral ties between India and Singapore have been enhanced by the opening of the Indian Centre in Singapore by Indian Union Commerce Minister Murasoli Maran and Singapore's Trade Minister George Yeo.[26] Supported by the Singapore Economic Development Board (EDB), the Jurong Town Corporation (JTC), the Federation of Indian Chambers of Commerce and Industry (FICCI) and the IndUS Entrepreneurs (TIE), the centre aims to facilitate start-ups and entrepreneurial companies from India. Minister Maran said that the Indian centre would help Indian companies to establish a presence in Singapore. This sentiment was echoed by Minister George Yeo, who said that in 1995 there were fewer than 50 Indian companies in Singapore but these have increased to 300 in 2001.[27] Singapore's Trade and Development Board (TDB) has also established overseas offices in various cities in India, like Chennai, New Delhi and Mumbai to foster greater economic linkages between the two countries.

TELECOMMUNICATIONS

The telecommunications sector in India apart from IT is one of the fastest growing sectors of the Indian economy. The number of lines and telephones in service has steadily increased between 1992 and 1996 (Table 2). With the introduction of the National Telecommunication Policy (NTP) of 1994 and 1999, India has sought to connect the most inaccessible and most remote villages and to reduce the costs of owning a telephone by providing consumers with a choice of private operators at competitive rates.

In Table 3 we can see the rate of teledensity in India as of 30 September 1999 which indicates that further improvement has been made in the telecom sector. This reflects the change that the Indian government has implemented since NTP 1999 and the increasing liberalization and deregulation of the telecom sector to allow foreign players to own up to 49 per cent of joint venture companies with their Indian counterparts. In Table 4 we have the teledensity in India in relation to its demography. The rate of teledensity is still relatively low.

TABLE 2: TELECOMS NETWORK DEVELOPMENT IN INDIA FROM 1992–6

Indicator	1992	1993	1994	1995	1996
Telephones in service (1000s)	6,706	7,713	8,877	10,588	12,892
Tel. lines per 100 popl.	0.77	0.88	0.99	1.15	1.38
New lines (1000s)	735	987	1,229	1,770	2,183
Lines in service (1,000s)	5,810	6,797	8,026	9,795	11,978
Lines in service per 100 popl.	0.67	0.77	0.89	1.07	1.28
Long-distance route km	94,476	107,462	122,957	142,113	168,633
No. of village telephones	74,404	10,4476	137,477	185,136	216,632
Local call pulses (billions)	29.8	40.1	46.7	58.6	78.5
Registered waiting list for telephones (1,000s)	2,289	2,845	2,497	2,153	2,277

Source: Department of Telecoms.

TABLE 3: INDIAN TELEDENSITY AS OF 30 SEPTEMBER 1999

Indicators	
Telephone Network	
Total No: Telephone Exchanges	25,400
Total Equipped Capacity (lines)	2,72,17,000
Total Working Connections (lines)	2,26,30,000
Total Public Telephones . . . (local, STD, highway)	5,73,055
Total Village Public Telephones	3,43,417

Source: Department of Telecoms.

TABLE 4: INDIAN TELEDENSITY AND RELATED DEMOGRAPHIC INFORMATION, AS OF APRIL 2002

Indicators	1997	1998
Telephone Network		
Main telephone lines in operation	1,78,02,000	2,15,94,000
Main telephone lines per 100 inhabitants	1.86	2.20
Residential main lines per 100 households	—	—
% digital main lines	99.9%	—
Waiting list for main lines	27,06,000	—
Demographics		
Population	95,52,20,000	98,22,23,000
Households	17,00,00,000	17,50,00,000
Gross domestic product (GDP; local currency)	15,636 (10 x 9)	

Source: *ITU Yearbook of Statistics—Telecommunication Services*, Chronological Time, Series: 1989–98.

The liberalization of the telecoms' sector has paved the way for foreign telecom companies like Singapore Telecoms (Sing Tel) to enter the Indian market. Sing Tel has collaborated with Bharti Enterprises of India to work on joint venture projects. In August 2001, Sing Tel had pumped US $400 million into Bharti for an effective 30 per cent share of the company's telecom stake.[28] One of their more ambitious projects is the building of a 11,800 km undersea fibre-optic cable (called Aquanet) to connect the Indian cities of Mumbai and Chennai to Singapore. The 50–50 joint-venture to build and operate one of the world's largest submarine cables would provide a big boost to the telecoms sector. Aquanet would provide users with a bandwidth of 8.4 terabits per second and would be able to accommodate 100 million telephone conversations simultaneously.[29]

INFRASTRUCTURE—PORTS DEVELOPMENT

The close economic cooperation between India and Singapore in infrastructure is also evident in the development and upgrading of Indian ports. With a coastline of 6,000 km, India has the potential to be a major shipping hub in the region if not internationally. The Port of Singapore Authority (PSA), a corporatized government company, has formed an alliance with South India Corporation (Agencies) Limited (SICAL) in order to bid for the upgrading, operation and maintenance of a berth at Tuticorin port in southern India.[30] The PSA was also interested in establishing joint ventures (JVs) with other Indian companies to develop ports in Chennai and Pipavav port in Gujarat. Through cooperation with the state government of Gujarat, PSA was able to upgrade the privatized Pipavav port. The PSA is in the process of converting Pipavav's existing three cargo berths into a full-fledged container terminal.

EMERGING ECONOMIC SECTORS

The sustainability of India and Singapore trade and economic linkages is not in doubt despite events such as the Asian Financial Crisis of 1997. Other economic sectors are being explored and assessed to find emerging areas that both countries could take advantage of for mutual benefit. These emerging sectors are predominantly in the services and R&D sectors and include financial, retail and health care services, as well as biotechnology and film production.

FINANCIAL SERVICES

Singapore's strategy to become a regional financial hub has been adversely affected by the regional economic downturn since the Asian financial crisis of 1997/8 and the region has not recovered fully from this phenomenon. As acknowledged by Singapore's new Finance Minister B.G. Lee Hsien Loong, the aftermath of the crisis had made it harder for Singapore to develop itself as a financial centre, 'because to be a financial centre you have to service a hinterland', and Singapore's immediate neighbours have decreased their demands for financial services from Singapore.[31] The alternative strategy, as mentioned by B.G. Lee is 'Singapore must therefore cast its net wider, to extend our catchment beyond our immediate neighbours.'[32]

B.G. Lee hinted that Singapore is looking into possible linkages with India in the financial sector. For example, Singapore is encouraging Indian technology companies to list here (Singapore) because it's 'closer, it's cheaper, and we have a market which is familiar with what's going on in India',[33] said B.G. Lee. The private banks have taken note of the deregulation that has started in the Indian financial sector and the growth of India's fast expanding middle class retail market. According to Hong Kong and Shanghai Banking Corporation's (HSBCs) deputy CEO in India, Chris Hothersall, 'expectations of India are very high in London and Hong Kong; we have got to widen our horizons'.[34]

With Indian state-owned banks having problems due to overstaffing and government interference, HSBC and other international banking giants like Citibank and Standard Chartered Grindlays have sensed opportunities in India's liberalized financial sector. HSBC group plans to invest more than US $75 million in India and has opened branches in Ahmedabad and Hyderabad, not to mention setting up an asset management company and a non-banking finance subsidiary.[35] In 1996, HSBC has also established an Indian Growth Fund at its branches in Singapore for investors.[36] The fund aims to achieve medium to long-term capital growth for its investors by investing primarily in securities. The securities are those listed on India's official stock exchange or traded in a regulated market.[37] Alternatively, investments would also be placed on companies that are closely linked to the growth and development of the Indian company.

India's top bank in Singapore, the Bank of India, has had a presence in Singapore for fifty years since 4 June 1951. The Bank of India had first started operations in a room at Raffles Hotel to provide banking services to the local Indian community.[38] It has 19 overseas branches including the one in Singapore at Hong Leong Centre which accounts for a third of its international revenue and employs some 82 people.[39] In return, one of Singapore's biggest banks, the Development Bank of Singapore, is hunting for suitable investments in India.[40] Singapore's capital market regulators have also asked Indian companies to get listed on its stock exchange. According to then Managing Director Tharman Shanmugaratnam of the Monetary Authority of Singapore, 'a critical mass of Indian companies that are not ready for the NYSE or NASDAQ could get listed on the Singapore Stock Exchange'.[41] Furthermore, by tapping the Singapore bond market, the Indian companies could diversify their financial portfolio.[42]

RETAIL SERVICES

The retail group, Dairy Farm International (DFI), which is part of the Hong Kong-based conglomerate, Jardine Matheson Holdings, has substantial retail interest in markets in South and South-East Asia, particularly in Singapore. The group has plans to establish up to 20 new Giant hypermarkets in the two regions from 2001–4;[43] for example, the Indian market will receive another three Giant hypermarkets to add to its current Giant hypermarket. DF is in a fortuitous position, being one of only three foreign players allowed into the retail sector in India. In 2000, with sales close to S $1 billion from its Singapore operations alone, DF intends to achieve a 'quantum leap' in the two regions through acquisition and organic growth.[44]

In Singapore, DFI has bought 130 stores since 1993. The 130 stores comprise well-known brand names such as 7-eleven convenience stores, Cold Storage supermarkets, Guardian Pharmacy chain and Photo Finish. In India, DFI entered the domestic market in 1996, with a local partner, RPG Spencer, to establish the first organized retail outlet in India.[45] DFI runs India's biggest retail supermarket and pharmacy chain with a total of 46 Foodworld markets in places like Bangalore, Chennai, Hyderabad and Pune. In addition, DFI also owns 17 Health and Glow pharmacy and beauty stores. According to DFI's regional director for South Asia, Michael Kok, 'the Indian market is absolutely huge and the plan is to increase the number of Foodworld outlets to 250 by 2005'. Kok also said that 'DFI and RPG Spencer have plans to form a joint venture to open India's first cash and carry outlet'. The proposed

50,000 sq. ft. store in Hyderabad will aim at trade buyers such as small retailers and restaurants. DFI owns 49 per cent of Foodworld and 50 per cent of Health and Glow.[46]

HEALTH CARE

Singapore leaders have spoken of the need to 'remake' Singapore's economy by promoting it as a regional hub service, such as for health care, education and tourism.[47]

The marketing aspects of this strategy would be to sell the Singapore brand name in areas like health care in the region to attract business from the region. The spin-offs from this would desirably be more value-added high paying jobs and possibly a better managed and funded health care system for Singaporeans as well. If justification was needed to show the lucrative potential of promoting health care services, it was estimated that the Mayo Clinic in the United States (one of the world's best) received S $5.5 billion in patient fees in 2001. This was more than Singapore's total spending on health care at S $4.7 billion in 2001.[48]

Singapore's health care services companies like the Raffles Medical Group, HMI Balestier Hospital and Parkway Holdings are also venturing to invest in other countries' health care services. For example, the HMI group will be establishing hospitals, medical centres, nurse training colleges and diagnostic laboratories in Malaysia, Indonesia, China, the Philippines and India.[49] Similarly, Parkway is also diverging from its traditional business of building hospitals towards more consulting and management work. Parkway had signed a 10-year consulting and management agreement to advise a group of investors who are building a private hospital in Vietnam's Ho Chi Minh City. Parkway is also negotiating a similar contract for a group of private investors in Bahrain in the United Arab Emirates.[50]

The staffing of these hospitals with qualified staff presented Parkway with a difficult problem because of Singapore's manpower constraints. To solve the problem, Parkway is negotiating to establish a joint-venture company with the Apollo Group of India, one of Asia's largest hospital and health care management companies.[51] Under this agreement, Parkway would secure hospital-management contracts around the region, while Apollo would provide the doctors, nurses, engineers and other qualified professionals needed to operate a hospital. Parkway also intends to offer training courses at its hospitals in Singapore before dispatching staff to its regional hospitals. Once these hospitals are established, upper level management positions would also need to be filled with qualified staff.[52] Apollo Hospitals complimented Parkway's plans to expand into the regional market because India's hospitals and health care sector is in the middle of a high growth phase because of its gradual corporatization in the 1990s. Apollo Hospitals, based in Chennai, was India's first corporate hospital in the 1980s.

BOLLYWOOD SINGAPORE?

Although India's Bollywood films have achieved world renown, Indian multimedia companies have started to collaborate with Singapore counterparts in film production. For example, Pentamedia Graphics (from India) have teamed up with the Economic Development (EDB) of Singapore to produce a full-length 2-D/3-D animated feature film titled *Buddha*.[53] Pentamedia's production crew will include 105 professionals based in Singapore. According to Pentamedia's chief operating officer, the 105 animation experts are specialists in areas such as 3-D backgrounds, effects animation, digital ink and paint.[54] Some of the animation experts will also have the opportunity to work in Pentamedia's studio in Chennai, India, while Pentamedia's own animators will travel to Singapore to work with and train local talent on the project.[55]

The animation film on the Buddha is a milestone in EDB's efforts to develop Singapore as a media hub and is part of the EDB's strategy to identify and promote new content creation capabilities in Singapore. According to EDB's Managing Director Ko Kheng Hwa, 'EDB's vision for the media industry is to build Singapore as a major media hub with global capabilities in content creation and reach'.[56] Kheng Hwa added that the film would not only spur the development of the animation industry here but is also a good example of international production companies tapping Singapore talent to produce their programmes. Overall, the media industry in Singapore now has 18 satellite broadcasters based here with more than 70 channel feeds for the Asian region and beyond.

India and Singapore have also collaborated in a number of Research and Development projects. Surprisingly, in the filmmaking sector, India's Bollywood has come to Singapore to advance the interests of both countries in this sector. Besides film making the next step would be for both countries to nurture linkages in the field of biotechnology.

BIOTECHNOLOGY

The establishment of the Bangalore IT Park also provides a suitable platform for India and Singapore to leverage on their mutual strengths to tap into the R&D potential in biotechnology. In early February 2002, the National University of Singapore (NUS) sent a delegation headed by its president Professor Shih Choon Fong to India, to learn from India's leading R&D organizations, like the Council of Scientific and Industrial Research (CSIR), the Indian Institute of Technology and the Centre for Biomedical Technology. Professor Shih said that the visit was an eye-opener and that NUS and Singapore had a lot to learn from these institutions (*The Straits Times*, 2 February 2002). He also added that despite shortcomings in infrastructure, this has not prevented research standards at these institutions from being globally competitive. Various factors that had contributed to the high quality of research in India included international benchmarking and the research culture.

Karnataka's Chief Minister, S.M. Krishna, had said that phase two of the Bangalore IT Park would be equipped to address the needs of R&D in biotechnology. The State's Minister for Medium and Large Industries, R.V. Deshpande, echoed the sentiment. He had invited Singapore businesses to consider moving beyond IT to biotech projects and pharmaceutical research (*The Straits Times*, 29 November 2000). The current importance of the biotechnology sector in India is reflected in the federal government's desire to ensure that the biotechnology revolution does not bypass the country.[57] Given Singapore's own emphasis for research in this area, this is fertile ground for both countries to increase their cooperation and exploit complementary strengths in this vital sector.

POTENTIAL UNLIMITED

The future of bilateral economic relations between India and Singapore is full of potential. Although the IT sector is the dominant sector in the trade linkages between both countries, other existing and emerging sectors have shown that the scope of bilateral economic ties extends beyond IT. The economies of both countries would be able to complement each other but this synergy has to be nurtured and developed for mutual benefit in a globalized trading system. With enhanced trade and economic linkages, India and Singapore would be better prepared to face the onslaught of economic globalization.

NOTES

1. Globalization is here defined as, 'the growing liberalization of international trade and investment and the resulting increase in the integration of national economies' by Daniel T. Griswold, in 'The Blessings and Challenges of Globalization', Center for Trade and Policy Studies, September 2001.
2. B.R. Nayar, *Globalization and Nationalism: The Changing Balance in India's Economic Policy, 1950–2000*, New Delhi, 2001, p. 15.
3. 'Globalise Your Economy, PM Goh Urges India', *Business Times*, 20 January 2000 and India 'must not reject globalisation', *The Straits Times*, Singapore, 20 January 2000.
4. As of July 2001, there are more than 130 bilateral and regional trade agreements in effect, most of which have come into being only in the 1990s. They are often called 'free trade agreements' (FTAs), or more accurately 'preferential trade agreements' (PTAs). These FTAs define mutual privileges that two countries promise each other in terms of market access, tariff reduction schemes and other exclusive benefits. These are applicable to defined trading spaces like the North American Free Trade Agreement (NAFTA), the ASEAN Free Trade Agreement (AFTA) or bilateral exchanges such as the Singapore–New Zealand FTA. Operating outside the jurisdiction of the multilateral trading system, these FTAs have their own internal rules, their own dispute settlement arrangements, and they are multiplying far faster than the World Trade Organization (WTO) can launch a new round of trade negotiations, see Yahya Faizal, 'Singapore-India: Possibilities of a Bilateral Free Trade Agreement?' (unpublished).
5. SAARC-South Asian Association for Regional Cooperation.
6. 'Focus/India and the Region: A New Day Dawns in the East', *Bangkok Post*, 10 March 2000.
7. Association of South-East Asian Nations—ASEAN
8. 'Wide Angle: Looking East', *The Statesman*, India, 25 November 2000.
9. Ibid.
10. 'Focus/India and the Region', *Bangkok Post*, 10 March 2000 and Faizal Yahya 'Of India's Economic Reforms and Uneven Playing Fields' (unpublished).
11. 'Wide Angle: Looking East', *The Statesman*, India, 25 November 2000.

12. 'Focus/India and the Region', *Bangkok Post,* 10 March 2000.
13. Nirmal Ghosh, 'New Delhi Acts on Look East Policy', *The Straits Times,* Singapore, 15 November 2000.
14. Ibid.
15. *Economic Linkages between Singapore and India: The IT Connection,* Singapore Ministry of Trade and Industry, November 2001.
16. Ibid.
17. Ibid.
18. Justin Doebele, 'What Bubble?' *Forbes Global,* 4 February 2001.
19. Ibid.
20. 'Venture Capital the Buzz', *Asia Today,* Sydney, May/June 2000.
21. The NSTB has invested in 21 funds and committed US $443 million. NSTB's partners include US based venture capitalists like Sequoia Capital, Doll Capital, Global Catalyst Partners, Crystal Internet Ventures, J.H. Whitney, Origin Partners, Warburg Pincus and Walden International, ibid.
22. The Temasek group of companies consists of major companies and encompasses a wide range of industries from manufacturing, financial and logistics to telecommunications and other services. The companies include DBS Bank, Orient Lines-APL, PSA Corporation, Singapore Airlines, Singapore Power and Singapore Telecom, among others.
23. Press Release–Temasek Holdings, 17 July 2001.
24. Ibid.
25. Ibid.
26. A. Baruah, 'Maran Inaugurates India Centre in Singapore', *The Hindu,* New Delhi, 13 October 2001.
27. Ibid.
28. Faizal Yahya, 'The Challenges of Globalization: Realising the Potential of Telecommunications in India' (unpublished).
29. Ibid.
30. Faizal Yahya, 'A Passage to India: Ports Development in India, the Singapore Connection' (unpublished).
31. Vikram Khanna, 'Cast Net Wider to Grow Financial Sector', *Business Times,* Singapore, 19 July 2001.
32. Ibid.
33. Ibid.
34. Sadanand Dhume, 'Banking: A Giant Awakens', *Far Eastern Economic Review,* 31 August 2000.
35. Ibid.
36. The HSBC Indian Growth Fund is a feeder fund that invests in the HSBC GIF Indian Equity Fund, a sub-fund of HSBC Global Investment Funds SICAV in Luxembourg and managed by HSBC Asset Management (Europe) Limited.
37. HSBC Indian Growth Fund Brochure.
38. Rachel Ong, 'BOI targets Net banking by Year-end', *Business Times,* Singapore, 2 June 2001.
39. Ibid.

40. R. Velloor, 'DBS Bank on the Prowl in India', *The Straits Times*, Singapore, 18 December 1999.
41. 'Indian Firms Urged to List on Singapore Exchange', *India Business*, India, 15 October 2001.
42. Ibid.
43. Colin Tan, 'Dairy Farm to Open 20 more Hypermarkets', *The Straits Times*, Singapore, 14 December 2001.
44. 'Indian Market Holds Promise', *The Business Times*, Singapore, 17 October 2000.
45. Ibid.
46. Ibid.
47. 'Health Care: Gunning for the Regional Pie', *The Straits Times*, Singapore, 14 December 2001.
48. Ibid.
49. 'South East Asian Health News', Issue 2, August 1997, *Business Development Asia.*
50. T. Saywell, 'Making House Calls, Health Care', *Far Eastern Economic Review*, 15 February 2001.
51. Ibid.
52. Ibid.
53. 'EDB in Buddha film tie-up', *Business Times*, Singapore, 7 June 2001.
54. 'EDB and Indian firm to make film on Buddha', *The Straits Times*, Singapore, 7 June 2001.
55. Ibid.
56. Ibid.
57. 'Partnerships, Not Piracy', *Far Eastern Economic Review*, 23 August 2001.

REFERENCES

Doebele, J., 'What bubble?', *Forbes Global*, 4 February 2001.

Dhume, S., 'Banking: A Giant Awakens', *Far Eastern Economic Review*, 31 August 2000.

Griswold, D.T., *The Blessings and Challenges of Globalization*, Center for Policy Studies, United States of America, June 2000.

Hong Kong and Shanghai Banking Corporation (HSBC), 'Indian Growth (Investment) Fund', brochure.

India Business, India, 15 October 2001.

Nayar, B.R., *Globalization and Nationalism, The Changing Balance in India's Economic Policy 1950–2000*, New Delhi: Sage Publications, 2001.

Report on Economic Linkages between Singapore and India: The IT Connection, Ministry of Trade and Industry, November 2001.

Saywell, T., 'Making House Calls, Health Care', *Far Eastern Economic Review*, 15 February 2001.

South East Asian Health News, Issue 2, *Business Development Asia*, August 1997.
Trade and Policy Studies, United States of America, September 2001.
Far Eastern Economic Review, 23 August 2001.
Asia Today, Sydney, May/June 2000.

NEWSPAPERS

Bangkok Post, Thailand, March 2000
Business Times, Singapore, June/July 2001
The Hindu, New Delhi, October 2001
The Statesman, India, November 2000
The Straits Times, Singapore, December 1999–December 2001

Jasjit Singh

Security after September Eleven

The world changed after 11 September 2001 in many ways and the contours of that change are not entirely clear as yet. It would be insufficient to describe the terrorist attacks on the United States as simple acts of terrorism driven, no doubt, by religious extremist ideology and the belief in violence as a means of dispute solving. Terrorism in various ways is as old as human conflict. It has been employed in various ways with the objective of imposing one's will on the other party through fear, as an old Chinese proverb says, to 'kill one and frighten ten thousand'. Large parts of the world have been the subject and object of terrorism during the second half of the twentieth century. Even the United States has been a target of international terrorism, in the attack on the World Trade Center in the early 1990s, in Oklahoma City, and in East Africa, Saudi Arabia, etc., in more recent years. We in India have been a conscious target of international terrorism for more than seventeen years. Many other examples can be cited. So what is different about 11 September?

What was witnessed by a large part of the world on that day was a live demonstration on the electronic media of suicide attacks with four hijacked civil airliners on the core elements of power of the sole superpower, namely, the financial and economic hub at the World Trade Center, the military headquarters at Pentagon of the most powerful military in the world, and no doubt the fourth aircraft heading toward the Capitol Hill, the symbol and seat of the world's most powerful democracy, if it had not crashed earlier. By definition a superpower must not be vulnerable to attack by any other power. It was this demonstrated vulnerability of the superpower that destroyed its image of invincibility. The impact has been even greater since the sole superpower had only a decade ago declared victory when the next most powerful state in the world had collapsed after more than four decades of confrontation and conflict. The impact was further intensified by the use of a novel method of simply flying hijacked unarmed civil airliners into the buildings with the clear intention not so much of killing a large number of people as of displaying the ability of the attacker to cause grievous harm to the state and society in the United States. The overall aim was no doubt to create a strong, possibly disproportionate, reaction to the act as well as broadcast to the people of the world the vulnerabilities of the modern state and society. If the core of the most powerful state in the world can be vulnerable to attack and destruction by groups of religious extremists, then surely all countries, especially liberal democracies, would remain even more vulnerable to the phenomenon of international terrorism.

The US response under the circumstances was to be expected except that what Washington, to its great credit, actually undertook was a much more calibrated response rather than a sledgehammer approach. In spite of the comparatively narrower concerns of each country there was not only global sympathy but also active cooperation with the United States in dealing with international terrorism. Special efforts were made to emphasize the proper dimensions of the problem as being international terrorism. Hence the war against the phenomenon, its leadership and infrastructure rather than a fight against Islam or any particular country.[1] India, with the world's second largest Muslim population, with its decades-old experience of transnational terrorism and of combating it, promptly offered full cooperation to the United States. And this provided a special impetus to the war against terrorism even by the Muslim countries. This is also the reason why President Bush's recent nomenclature of Iran, Iraq and North Korea as an 'axis of evil' came under criticism even from US allies.

THE THIRD WORLD WAR?

Given the nature of events that led to 11 September and even more what has followed, it is possible to hypothesize that the fateful day of September 2001 marked the beginning of a virtual Third World War. This is a war distinctly different from the earlier World Wars, but still total in nature and perhaps even more vicious since the target of one adversary in that war are the innocents of the world. The war is not against a particular country, religion or civilization but against a phenomenon which has its roots in a combination of diverse factors. This is not to suggest that countries and their governments, religious groups and ideology, or other factors like the Cold War and its debris in the shape of a phenomenal spread of weapons of military specifications into civil society, have not played a crucial part in promoting or prosecuting terrorism, but to acknowledge that the implications extend far beyond the national boundaries. In fact the war against the Soviet Union in Afghanistan played a crucial role in shaping the current war. The nature of change in war has been clearly discernible in recent decades although the tendency was to see it in essentially national terms. But if we probe beyond the immediate and nationalist perceptions a couple of mega-trends can be identified which would make this war not all that easy to win even if the international community finally gets down to fighting it out. A number of such factors are briefly examined here to focus on the security challenges and policy options that the international community faces.

First, asymmetry has always played a crucial role in warfare. With modern means of warfare and the heightened vulnerability of states to conventional war, the probability of such wars has been reducing. During the Cold War the two superpowers and their allies conducted numerous 'proxy wars' essentially as the means of indirect warfare. But most such wars were being fought on the basis of generating asymmetry. The Viet Cong against the United States in Vietnam and the Mujahideen against the Soviet Union in Afghanistan are prime examples. Ideology played a key role in both cases. In the first case the ideology was based on communism while in the latter case religion was promoted as the ideological foundation (against the Communist Soviet Union). As it is ideology played an increasing role in warfare during the twentieth century. Introduction and support of religion-based ideology of the Mujahideen (and the implicit militant *jehad* in the name of Islam) by the United States through Pakistan as the "front-line state' marked a major change in the strategy and tactics of the asymmetric warfare for political goals.

Second, efforts to legitimize the use of religion for political goals and violence in the name of religion were underway in Pakistan well before even the first Afghanistan war of the 1980s. In fact the use of terror in the name of religion itself had been sought since the 1970s. One of the prime examples of the legitimacy of terrorism has come from Pakistani military leadership that has been running the country during most of its existence. Pakistani leadership not only introduced greater Islamization in society after 1971, but its military leadership actively sought to rationalize the use of terror as being sanctified by religion.[2] As Pakistan moved towards greater Islamization in the 1970s, it also sought increased inspiration from religion for its strategic doctrine. General Zia, as the head of state and the army, encouraged such efforts. Brigadier S.K. Malik has (fundamentally erroneously) interpreted the Holy Koran in search for guidelines, and has placed a strong emphasis on the interpretation that the Holy Koran enjoins upon the believers to use terror as a weapon of war. 'The Quranic military strategy,' Malik wrote, 'thus enjoins us to *prepare ourselves for war to the utmost in order to strike terror into the hearts of the enemies, known or hidden, while guarding ourselves from being terror-stricken by the enemy*' (emphasis in original).[3] The book teaches that terror must be struck during the preparatory stage, in the run up to war, during war, and for war termination. Terror struck into the hearts of the enemies, therefore, 'is not only a means, it is the end in itself. Once a condition of terror into the opponent's heart is obtained, hardly anything is left to be achieved. It is the point where the means and the ends meet and merge.' Later, Army Chief General Aslam Beg and other army leaders inevitably quoted these conclusions to exhort the officers when addressing them, especially at the senior training establishments.

The result has been to alter the classical Clausewitzean doctrine that war is an extension of politics by other means to a new prescription that war through terror would be an instrument of politics and foreign policy/military strategy by other (non-diplomatic and non-military) means. The external role in violence inside another state has been increasing. Distinction between domestic terrorism and international terrorism has been diffusing due to greater external involvement in internal terrorist violence in a country. Today there is hardly any significant domestic armed conflict that does not actively receive political support, weapons, substantive financial assistance and safe havens beyond the borders where terrorist acts are committed.

Terrorism is shifting from its traditional political orientation to religious-ideology driven violence. Compared to their near absence three decades ago, today religious groups constitute over two-thirds of the militant/terrorist entities in the world. Ideological reasons had driven the Cold War and its hot segment, the proxy wars. Toward the end of the Cold War religion was increasingly exploited for political and ideological purposes, especially in Afghanistan, to provide motivation for war and violence. The nearly two-decades old war in Afghanistan was fuelled and sustained by religion-based ideological factors—domestic, regional, and global. Religion is coming to play an increasing role in politics even in states that have pursued liberal democratic or socialist ideologies. International security is consequently affected seriously, because '. . . the combination of religion and politics is potentially explosive. The combination of religion and nationalism is stronger, but a blend of the three has an extremely destructive potential.'[4]

The result has been that war has undergone some fundamental changes in recent decades. The risks and consequences of a nuclear war remain with us as long as such weapons are not eliminated. Conventional wars are no longer viable since the basic rationale of territory as a source of material and manpower resources as in earlier periods has been almost totally eroded by changed political dimensions provided by de-colonization, democracy and the high political awareness of populations. The economic means of production also are no longer dependent upon natural resources (except for oil and gas) as in earlier periods. Traditional conventional war therefore has become less likely. Even when fought it would have a limited impact beyond the military forces except where the political and economic costs of that war become high. For this reason, rather than territory per se, conventional wars would remain in vogue for a long time.

But the real change taking place is the shift of warfare to the sub-conventional level. The chief characteristics of this change are outlined in Table 1.

TABLE 1: EFFECTS OF SHIFT OF WARFARE TO SUB-CONVENTIONAL LEVEL

Type of War	Probability of War	Target and Effect
Nuclear war	Least probable	Predominantly innocents Maximum destruction
Conventional war	Low probability	Military combatants Limited effects
Sub-conventional war (especially through terrorism)	High probability	Predominantly innocents Democracies and liberal society particularly vulnerable Very high politico-psychological impact

Note: In each case asymmetry enhances the probability of war and its impact with very high political (and human) costs for the loser.

VULNERABILITY OF STATE AND SOCIETY

September 11 has once again demonstrated, if indeed any demonstration was needed, that the *vulnerability of the modern state has been increasing especially through the threat and use of violence against civilians*. This is primarily due to the vulnerability of the civil society to violence. Unarmed civilians were always vulnerable to violence and this has been a major reason for creation and maintaining of armed forces, whether police or military, of the state so that the institution can provide collective security to individual citizens. Wars for territories are now obsolete for a variety of reasons, but paradoxically that has increased the vulnerabilities of society. Modern society requires people to function in an integrated manner and their dependence on institutions and infrastructure naturally increases with development and progress. The higher the quality of life in a society, the higher is the level of interdependence on different elements and sub-systems for keeping that society functioning efficiently. For example, a modern state is highly vulnerable even to conventional war. Europe has hundreds of nuclear power reactors on stream on any one day, and a couple of million tons of chemicals may be on the move by train or road. A conventional attack could produce numerous Chernobyls and Bhopal tragedies. On the other hand, military technology has been making war a far more expensive proposition and the re-supply of weapons and military equipment places severe constraints on the ability of nations to go to war. Asymmetry therefore is found in the application of force and violence in more indirect ways. Terrorism has been one of the ways in which wars are being fought. And 11 September was symbolic of that war.

Liberal society and democratic states are especially vulnerable to terrorist violence because of the contradictory requirements of protecting freedom and human rights on one side and exercising tighter measures and controls against violence on the other. On the other hand, democracies by their very nature are the most vulnerable to international terrorism but are also the best qualified to deal with international terrorism. However they have also been the most reluctant (at least till 11 September 2001) to take assertive action against terrorism because of the need to balance concerns for liberty and human rights.

VIOLENCE AGAINST CIVILIANS

The problems have been compounded with the targeting of civilians. Although concerns about civilian casualties have started to emerge, for a variety of reasons targeting of civilians had been increasingly legitimized during the past two centuries. Starting from the Napoleonic Wars to the First World War, populations were not only increasingly incorporated in wars, but also started to become their prime targets. Released of earlier limitations of having to necessarily destroy the adversary's military or first conquer his territory, air warfare made it possible to target the adversary nation's society (and hence its 'will') directly. Early attempts to control the process failed. On the other hand the strategists of Western Europe and the USA conceptualized that air power will project the spear point of a nation's military force behind the frontlines of the battlefield (and thus escape the horrors and costs of trench warfare) into an enemy's vital areas to render it powerless to defend itself. Aerial bombing would cause such destruction and paralysis that 'resistance is no longer possible and capitation is the outcome'. [5] The essential target was the enemy nation. Douhet was forthright about inflicting *terror from the skies* when he prophesied[6] that victory 'must depend upon smashing the material and moral resources of a people caught in a frightful cataclysm which haunts them everywhere without cease till the final collapse of all social organisation'.[7] As technology advanced and matured, this was manifested in the 'strategic' bombings of Second World War, with the killing of people during the bombing of Dresden, the decimation of Coventry, the fire-bombing of Tokyo, and the final culmination in Hiroshima and Nagasaki. Society had become totally inclusive to war in the total war paradigm. Nuclear strategies, with the potential of mass destruction and nuclear winter, have perpetuated the paradigm since then.

While the trends of the past two centuries had made society inclusive to war, the trends of the past four decades are, in addition, making war inclusive to society. Expansion of war (and violent conflict) in social depth is one of the most serious challenges to the democratic principle, society and peace (and hence prosperity and progress).

At the same time terrorism has come to be increasingly used as an instrument of politics and foreign policy. This is a pernicious reversal of a çivilized approach to dispute settlement in general and the current trend of democratization and cooperative security in the world in particular. Its effectiveness has been increasing because of the ever-greater vulnerabilities of modern society to acts of terrorism where liberal democracies are especially at risk from this method of application of violent force.

Transnational crime has created tremendous opportunities for international terrorism to be pursued at a scale and reach which was earlier not possible. It needs to be noted that two of the world's three largest narcotics producing and exporting regions are also located in the same region (in fact contiguous to India's borders on the West, which has been the epicentre of international terrorism, as well as to the East). Both Singapore and India have a common stake in reversing the trend. The linkage between transnational crime, especially narcotics trafficking and terrorism is deep. The growth of narcotics and its trade has been a major factor in sustaining terrorism across the world. A brief selective list can give an idea of the issues and scale involved:

- Annual profits from global narcotics and other transnational crime is roughly estimated to be equal to $500 billion, that is, equal to 2 per cent of global GDP.
- As many as $500 billion criminal dollars went through the US banking system in 1997.
- Based on the estimates of current value of drug money and its compound growth its value would reach $1,500 billion by AD 2014, that is, equal to the value of the world stock of gold.
- In April 1994 INTERPOL Secretary General Raymond Kendall, talking about drug trafficking in the hands of organized crime, stated that 'INTERPOL has a file of 250,000 major criminals, 200,000 of whom are tied to drug trafficking. . . .'
- Over 560 cases of nuclear fissile material smuggling were reported from the Soviet Union between 1991–5.
- In late 1995 and again in April 1996 a German train transporting nuclear fuel on the Hamburg-Hanover railway line was derailed by explosion.

The result of the above trends has been that the centre of gravity of international terrorism has been shifting from the Middle East toward South Asia with Afghanistan-Pakistan as its epicentre.

RESPONSE OPTIONS

There are three broad issues that require consideration in formulating specific policy choices:

First, globalization has expanded and deepened the scope and extent of opportunities for terrorism that spans the globe now. One has only to look at the international connections and linkages of the actors in the 11 September attacks to grasp the scale and extent of global networking. By the same logic the challenge cannot be adequately met by national measures alone. The phenomenon of international terrorism by definition requires coordinated international responses while each country has to undertake specific measures of its own. This has been the major fall-out of 11 September when the United States and most of the countries realized that 'there are no good terrorists and bad terrorists'. There are just terrorists especially those driven by ideology based on religious extremist beliefs and understanding.

Second, imperatives of international cooperation require that the international order itself be vectored toward a more cooperative world. Non-violence is the centrepiece of such cooperation. The central conclusion is that while multipolarity within the Western alliance system exists (which makes this construct unipolar in the global context), the international order is inexorably moving toward greater democratization and plurality. The more prominent characteristics of the emerging international order are listed in Table 2.

A far more plural international order as compared to the Cold War period already exists. The challenge ahead of the international

TABLE 2: INTERNATIONAL ORDER: COMPARATIVE CHARACTERISTICS

Bipolar	Polycentric
Predictable, rigid	Unpredictable, flexible
Confrontation or cooperation related to Cold War	Concurrent cooperation and confrontation based on national interests
Ideology-based foreign and security policy	Functional policies
Hegemonic	Non-hegemonic
Eurocentric	Asia-centred

community is how to vector and expedite the environment toward a non-polarized non-hegemonic plural system with a degree of assurance that reversal (including to a bilateral Cold War) does not take place. A large number of measures and issues will need to be considered in assessing the direction and progress toward such a goal. But in essence we need to ensure that polycentricity, which is already taking strong roots, should be encouraged and the future international order should be built toward strengthening polycentricity rather than allowing it to drift toward any form of polarity.

Third, democracy, especially the deepening of the democratic principle and practice is the best guarantee against violence and its export. Terrorism is nothing but unabashed aggression and oppression. It fractures society and the community in ways and means that any other armed crime cannot do. International terrorism in addition vitiates international relations, expanding the threat envelope in a variety of ways. By spreading fear and terror it not only tends to compel acquiescence by the common citizen to the actions of the terrorists but it also generates anger and the emotion of revenge. Terrorism erodes institutions especially in a democratic country and undermines the confidence of the people in the state, especially in the democratic principle. Above all it promotes a culture of violence, as opposed to a culture of non-violence and tolerance so critical to civilized and inclusive society. This rapidly leads to erosion of institutions of civil society. There are a series of measures that would be needed to tackle the rising phenomenon of international terrorism. It is not intended to cover them in detail here. These steps require international cooperation, regional action and a multifaceted national policy that addresses all the issues involved that allow terrorism to take root.

But the central point to be recognized is that the logic and essence of emerging international terrorism is based on religious extremist ideology. And this is not the prerogative of one particular religion or the other. A religious sect in an otherwise peaceful society of Japan had suddenly launched a chemical weapon attack on the Tokyo subway in March 1995. If the aim of causing 40,000 deaths was not achieved (only 12 died), it was more due to sheer coincidence of an aerosol not functioning rather than any benign sentiment of the terrorists. We have to recognize—and emphasize firmly and publicly—that terrorism, especially that prosecuted in the name of religious ideology, directly and fundamentally targets and threatens the ideology on which a liberal, free democratic society is built.

The core of the strategy of response to terrorism therefore must rest on the ideological dimension. This can only be constructed on the democratic principle. Values based on the concept of equality of the human being and the right to pursue a life without fear and in peace must define the central goal of human endeavour.

Empirical evidence now exists that regardless of their capabilities, power, GDP, or cultural correlates, democracies indulge in the least amount of foreign violence.[8] This by definition would be as true of a state as of a society and a community which are cooperative, consultative and tolerant. They are therefore least likely to indulge in war, traditional or unconventional, against other democracies. It has to be remembered that democracy is a method of non-violence. It institutionalizes ways of solving disputes and disagreements over fundamental questions by promoting a culture of negot-iations, concessions, tolerance and even a willingness to lose with the hope of winning another day. Democracy however cannot be achieved simply by legislation although legislation is a great asset in strengthening the norms and culture of democracy. Imagine the history of our subcontinent if Mohammed Ali Jinnah's famous address to the Constituent Assembly (on 11 August 1947) of the newly emerging Pakistan had been codified in its constitution at an early stage! But this would still have required the values and norms to be nurtured and carefully protected from the vagaries and failings of human nature.

At the same time it needs to be emphasized that peace is to be expected at the end though the process of democratization may in fact create more violence than even stable authoritarian and totalitarian regimes. The case of Pakistan after 1985 is symptomatic. It is the period when democracy and its institutions are fragile that the greatest care has to be taken about the unleashing of violence and terror in pursuit of narrow ideological and political goals often escalated by domestic tensions within the power structure.

For us in India ideology has been clearly spelt out in the founding principles of our Constitution and these must remain as the core of our ideology. The ideological struggle against the exclusiveness implicit in those who pursue and promote terrorism would, by the nature of things, be a long haul. But the length of the struggle would also be determined by the resolve with which a democratic society pursues its own ideological goals.

NOTES

1. Even in the case of the war in Afghanistan, it was often ignored that the Taliban regime was a rebel regime that usurped power through violent means, supported from across the borders by Pakistan.
2. For example, General Zia ul-Haq as the Chief Marshal Law Administrator wrote the foreword recommending the book written by Brigadier S.K. Malik of the Pakistan Army in late 1970s who argued, in a self-serving misinterpretation, that the Holy Koran teaches the use of terror as a weapon against the enemy. See S.K. Malik, *The Quranic Concept of War*, Lahore: Wajidalis, 1979, pp. 58–9. Stephen Cohen had argued that Pakistani military officers on courses in the United States over the years were more interested in studying guerrilla warfare from the perspective of waging it (unlike the American officers who study it to learn how to combat it). See Stephen Cohen, *The Pakistan Army*, New Delhi: Himalayan Books, 1984, p. 34.
3. S.K. Malik, *The Quranic Concept of War*, Lahore: Wajidalis, 1979, pp. 58–9.
4. Falih Abd al Jabbar, 'The Gulf War and Ideology: The double-edged sword of Islam', in Haim Bresheeth and Nira Yuval-Davis (eds.), *The Gulf War and the New World Order*, London: Zed Books, 1991, p. 217.
5. W.F. Craven and J.B. Cate (eds.), *The Army Air Forces in World War II*, Chicago: University of Chicago Press, 1948.
6. A prophecy that was played out tragically on 11 September.
7. Lee Kennett, *A History of Strategic Bombing*, New York: Charles Scriber, 1982.
8. R.J. Rummel, *Power Kills: Democracy as a Method of Non-Violence*, London: Transaction Publishers, 1997.

Bilveer Singh

Security Issues in South-East Asia: A Singaporean Perspective

INTRODUCTION

By the early 1980s, security analysts were convinced that some sort of a 'security community' was in existence among the original members of the Association of South-East Asian Nations (ASEAN), with certain common rules and norms being in existence, and more important, the existence of a resolve to settle disputes peacefully without resort to the use of force. Scholars spoke of a South-East Asian 'regional complex', an 'emerging security community' and even more important, the acceptance of a 'code of conduct', best testified by the endorsement of the South-East Asian Treaty of Amity and Cooperation.

Despite this, mutual suspicions and inter-states tensions have continued unabated among countries in the region. This was driven by the underlying fault lines of diverse and competing national interests, ethnicity, religion, unsettled border disputes, differing threat perceptions, latent suspicions and differing approaches towards the Great Powers. In this regard, Singapore's security outlook was no exception, with its primary concern being its two immediate neighbours, namely, Malaysia and Indonesia, with whom bilateral relations have see-sawed, particularly with the former. Even though Singapore's relations with Indonesia from 1974 to 1997 were largely cordial, in many ways, Malaysia and Indonesia have continued to preoccupy the security planners in Singapore and the insecurity dilemma has somewhat worsened as the Republic entered the new millennium.

As contentious bilateral relations in the region have been saturated by various studies, this paper will not focus on bilateral relations but cast the Republic's security outlook wider by focusing on ASEAN as a whole.[1] Since ASEAN's formation in August 1967 and particularly since the American defeat in Indo-China in 1975, Singapore has viewed its foreign policy as being closely intertwined with the regional organization. While in the early years Prime Minister Lee Kuan Yew and his government were somewhat skeptical of ASEAN's value, best evident from Lee's frequent visits to the US and Europe rather than the region, this changed perceptibly from the mid-1970s. Following the Cambodian crisis in the late 1970s and the various trials and tribulations that ASEAN underwent and successfully overcame, ASEAN, today, for all intents and purposes, has become the cornerstone of Singapore's foreign policy. Singapore's attitude and orientations were further reinforced by the end of the Cold War that transformed an expanded ASEAN into a positive force in regional and world politics. Even though ASEAN appears to be suffering a crisis of identity, with many skeptics questioning its future usefulness, Singapore has, however, continued to champion ASEAN and its relevance in regional and world politics. This mainly stems from the determining factors of Singapore's foreign policy as well as the belief that Singapore, the South-East Asian region as well as the world as a whole will be worst off without an effective and functioning ASEAN.

Against this backdrop, this paper aims to undertake the following:

(1) Briefly examine the key imperatives behind Singapore's foreign and defence policies.
(2) Analyse Singapore's view and role in ASEAN, especially in the light of the various challenges the regional organization has been facing since the 1997 Asian Financial Crisis.
(3) Examine Singapore's response to the challenge posed by the terrorist attack on 11 September 2001 and how it has complicated the Republic's security outlook.

KEY DETERMINANTS OF SINGAPORE'S FOREIGN POLICY[2]

History: Singapore believes that historically it has been part of the South-East Asian region, particularly the 'Malay World'. Before the British excised Singapore for the Crown, Singapore was effectively part of the Riau Lingga Empire, particularly the state of Johor.

In many ways, the 'Malay World' remains geopolitically, geo-economically and geo-socially vital for the survival of Singapore.

Geography: What makes Singapore's historical connection with the region a reality is its geography. Located in the heart of South-East Asia, three geographical realities have shaped Singapore's outlook. First, being the smallest and only city-state in the region has particularly shaped its sense of vulnerability. Second, its location at the crossroads of east-west, north-south communications between the Indian and Pacific Oceans, especially controlling the choke points along the Straits of Malacca and Singapore, has been particularly important. Third and finally, being sandwiched between Malaysia in the north and Indonesia in the south has largely circumscribed Singapore's manoeuvrability as a state and implies that geographical 'border pressures' from these two states are vital in determining Singapore's outlook.

Demography: Singapore's history and geography is accentuated by its unique demographic make-up. Although it is located in the heart of South-East Asia and particularly the 'Malay World', Singapore's population is made up of a Chinese majority. In 2000, the population breakdown was: 76.8 per cent Chinese, 13.9 per cent Malays, 7.9 per cent Indians and 1.4 per cent others. In other words, Singapore is effectively a 'Chinese island' in a 'Malay Sea'. How to survive in this demographic adversity, especially where it is an extreme minority is one of the key challenges confronting Singapore and its foreign policy.

Economic: The geographic and demographic challenges have been further reinforced by the fact that even though Singapore has performed extremely well economically, it still remains largely dependent upon the outside world, including its South-East Asian neighbours for its basic food, raw materials, markets and investments. Even though it has performed remarkably well in the economic arena, it remains sensitive and vulnerable as it is greatly subjected to the economic cycles of the world in turn, which can affect the political, economic and social health of Singapore.

Strategic: What has also been important in Singapore's outlook has been the importance of South-East Asia to the great powers. Due to the region's resource treasure house, its control of vital sea-lanes of communications and its proximity to important centres of power in China, Japan and India, the region has always attracted the attention of the great powers that have developed enduring interests in the region. To that extent, the survival of Singapore is also closely intertwined with the policies and actions of the great powers.

The combination of these imperatives has shaped Singapore's foreign policy outlook, largely exuding insecurity. As part of its policy to survive and promote the well-being of its populace, the adoption of a wise and prudent foreign policy has always been a key thrust of the Singapore leadership. There is also the realization that Singapore's future is closely linked up with that of the region. Hence, the pro-active involvement and stakes of Singapore in the region, particularly ASEAN. This was, however, affected by the shift of paradigm brought about by the end of the Cold War. This has had a number of implications for the region that, in turn, affected Singapore's outlook towards the region.

The end of the Cold War created a situation of flux with uncertainty as the key characteristic.[3] The bipolar Cold War order was replaced by a new paradigm, characterized, among others, by:

- Shift from bipolarity to multi-polarity
- Shift from external aggression to internal instability
- Shift from geo-strategy to geo-economics
- Shift from competitive to cooperative security
- Rise of ethno-nationalism and religious strife
- Rise of regional powers

In the South-East Asian arena, the end of the Cold War led to a number of developments:

- The diminishing role and influence of the US and Russia
- Growing assertiveness of ASEAN in regional and international politics
- Emergence of a seeming 'no power vacuum' situation in the region in spite of the phasing out of the superpower rivalries
- Greater interactions among South-East Asian countries
- Greater economic assertiveness of the Great Powers in South-East Asia

- Rapid economic growth of South-East Asia
- Greater assertiveness of the Asian powers in South-East Asia and worldwide

It is against this backdrop and development that Singapore's South-East Asian challenge should be viewed and understood.

SINGAPORE AND THE SOUTH EAST ASIAN CHALLENGE

While the ASEAN region was dubbed a 'miracle' by outside observers, this changed perceptibly following the outbreak of the Asian financial crisis in August 1997. The financial crisis led to the economic 'meltdown' of the regional economies. Not only did this consume and bring about the downfall of the governments in Bangkok and Jakarta; it also unleashed political and social instability in the region. Many saw this as the return of South-East Asia to its traditional epitaph of instability. Here, particularly important was the crisis of leadership in Indonesia as well as its ensuing economic and social-cultural meltdown.

As a consequence of the socio-political and economic crises unleashed by the Asian financial crisis, the ASEAN region faced the following challenges:

- Overcome the political and economic crises facing the region in transition.
- Reverse the regional and international media emphasis of bad news on ASEAN.
- Reverse negative market assessments and foreign investors' disinvestments from ASEAN, especially from South-East Asia to North-East Asia.
- Emphasize that the 'East Asian Miracle' was not a 'Mirage'.
- Ensure that ASEAN did not disappear from the radar screen of the developed countries, especially the US.

Singapore's Response

Due to the high stakes Singapore has in the ASEAN region and the close manner in which its own political and economic survival is intertwined with that of the region, the Republic has responded in a largely pragmatic fashion to ensure that ASEAN remains relevant and important to its members and the world community at large. Singapore's response could be seen in various policies it undertook at home, in the region and the world at large. These included:

(a) Restructuring and strengthening the political, economic and social-cultural resilience of the Republic in order to be able to weather the shocks from without. The restructuring of the banking sector in the country is a case in point, just as is its continued emphasis on productivity, information technology and the encouraging of high-technology industries into the country.

(b) Continuing to emphasize the importance of ASEAN in regional and global geopolitics. This is undertaken through the following means:

- (i) Emphasize that the collective, political and economic power of ASEAN remains invaluable.
- (ii) Stress that ASEAN provides a unique framework to constrain centrifugal forces that could destabilize the region.
- (iii) Emphasize that ASEAN is simply too important for global powers and that it is only a matter of time before ASEAN rebounces.
- (iv) Stress that countries in the region are undergoing change and it is only a matter of time before they recover and come out stronger.
- (v) That it is in the strategic interest of the great powers to see ASEAN successful and healthy.
- (vi) That any negative development in ASEAN would directly impact upon the other regions, especially North-East Asia, South Asia and the South Pacific.
- (vii) Emphasize ASEAN's value as it allowed for all kinds of engagements in the wider region, best manifested by the Post-Ministerial Conference, ASEAN Free Trade Agreement, Asia-Pacific Economic Conference, ASEAN Regional Forum, Asia-Europe Meeting, ASEAN Investment Area and ASEAN + 3 meeting.
- (viii) Emphasize that any prolonged weakening of ASEAN would make China's hegemony in the region a reality to the detriment of all regional and global powers and the best way to

pre-empt this was to ensure that the Western powers, especially the US, do not detach themselves from the region.

Over and above these policies and emphases, Singapore also tried to project itself as a 'healthy and successful' state in the region. Here, even though Singapore had some detractors in the ASEAN region, the goal was to demonstrate to the outside world that not all was bad in the ASEAN region. This was undertaken by Singapore's attempt to differentiate itself from the region. Thus, even though many countries were in political and economic turmoil, Singapore was not only stable but also performing well economically. To that extent, it could anchor the interests of the external economies so that it could work out a win-win formula. The bilateral Free Trade Agreements that Singapore worked out with the US, Australia, New Zealand, Japan, Canada, Mexico and a number of Latin American countries such as Chile was part of this endeavour.

Limitations

Despite these efforts there were and are clear limits to what Singapore can and cannot do. First, Singapore cannot escape from what was and is happening in the ASEAN region and as long as instability prevails, it will continue to have a spillover effect, like undermining international confidence in the South-East Asian region, among others. Here, Singapore's political and strategic fortunes will be determined by the manner in which ASEAN develops. Presently, it has been weakened by: (a) the weakened position of individual members, (b) inward orientation of various members due to internal problems, (c) membership of weak and poor new states, (d) the inability to cooperate on a region-wide basis, (e) the negative image the media has given ASEAN since 1997, and most important of all, (f) the loss of Indonesian leadership since the fall of Suharto in May 1998. At the same time, developments in Malaysia and Indonesia will continue to have a direct impact on Singapore's outlook and future. To that extent, the insecurity dilemma continues. Also, the sheer limit that the maximum power it can mobilize is that of a city-state, albeit a successful one, is also a telling factor that when it comes to the crunch, there is not that much that it can do except through cooperation with other powerful states. As such, Singapore continues to be at the mercy of its 'big and powerful friends' as well as the goodwill of other like-minded nations.

Additionally, over and above the limits imposed by the fact that Singapore is a vulnerable small city-state, largely a Chinese island and greatly dependent on the outside world for its existence, two other factors will also be important. First, how Singapore comes to terms with the generational change of leadership in the region, particularly in the post-Mahathir and post-Gus Dur era. Can Singapore really 'remake' positively its relations with its immediate neighbours and if so, in what directions? Can trust ever exist between Singapore and its immediate neighbours, especially in the light of the various geopolitical realities? Second, how Singapore adjusts to the emergence of the Asia-Pacific region as a strategic, political and economic centre of gravity of the world, the increasing instability brought about by the Sino-American tensions as well as the problems posed by global terrorism, will be an equally daunting task.

Singapore's Continued Commitment to Asean

Despite these challenges, Singapore continues to fly the ASEAN flag. Why? The following can be posited as the main reasons:

—It is in the best interest of the city-state and the region to do so.
—Singapore has the legitimacy and credibility to portray the potential of ASEAN.

Here, Singapore has not just spoken about it but actualized it through various policies. In the past, when it spoke of the importance of American military presence in the region, it showed the way by providing facilities for the American Air Force and Navy. Now, the Free Trade Areas are almost the economic variant of the American military facilities. As long as the Western economic powers can be convinced of this policy, this would imply that they would remain engaged and committed to the region and in the final analysis, ASEAN will remain on the radar screen of these giant political and economic players.

DEVELOPMENTS AND CHALLENGES SINCE 11 SEPTEMBER 2001

As Singapore is very closely intertwined with the global strategic, political and economic grid, there are not that many countries that are more sensitive to shifts in the international paradigm in their foreign and defence policies as is Singapore. Integrating closely into the world economy and viewing it as a 'global city' has been an important plank of its security and growth. Its strategic outlook has always been shaped by the balance of power obtaining in the international system at any one time. As such, when the World Trade Center and the Pentagon were attacked on 11 September 2001 and the United States responded with a policy of countries being 'with or against us', there was an immediate impact on Singapore's strategic outlook, all the more when this took place against a backdrop of an economic slow-down worldwide.

The terrorist attack of 11 September 2001 greatly impacted upon the security outlook of Singapore and this can be best examined at three levels, namely, international, regional and national.

International

Prior to the 11 September attack, the United States was championing democracy and human rights, and it was only in the later part of Clinton's second Administration that greater attention was being paid to economic cooperation. 11 September changed all this. The Republicans under Bush, already converts of *real politik* and in some ways, carry-overs of the 'Cold War' mentality, saw the challenge in such a term and re-oriented American foreign policy in a new direction. In a way, there appears to be a new 'Cold War', only this time, the enemy is not 'international communism' but 'international terrorism'. The fight against terrorism is being conducted almost in a Cold War fashion with the key question being as to how long Washington and its allies would be able to sustain this war.

While Singapore had always seen the triangular relations between the United States, Japan and China as being the most critical in the Asia-Pacific region, and was most concerned with tensions among the three key players, especially Sino-US relations, an important consequence of 11 September has been the seeming warming of Sino-American ties and the greater convergence between the two as far as the threat of international terrorism is concerned. At the same time, however, the US seems to be resuming its military build-up albeit slowly in the Asia-Pacific region, best evident in its initial deployment of more than 600 personnel in the Philippines. There is also the potential of China's concern about the real intentions of the US as far as the 'military encirclement' and 'containment' of China is concerned. Notwithstanding this, the Sino-American convergence in counter-terrorism provides a unique window of opportunity for the co-option into the 'strategic loop' of India, with New Delhi being increasingly viewed as a key player in this anti-terrorist 'coalition' as India has been subjected to this scourge for a long time.

Internationally, Singapore supported the various counter-terrorism measures that were being undertaken, especially by the US and its allies. Singapore condemned the 11 September attack as an attack on the 'civilized world'. She has strongly supported retaliation against the perpetrators, as she believes that there is no safety in silence. Singapore's leaders defended their support for the US on the following grounds:

> We have to stand up for our principles. It's not an attack just on the US. It's 7,000-odd casualties, and more than 2,000 were from 80 different countries. So it's an attack on all civilized, open countries in the world. Singapore is also vulnerable. We are a financial centre, we are an economic hub, we are an open city. It happened in the US. We can take precautions but we can never say it will not happen in Singapore. And indeed, such things have happened in Singapore.[4]

In the same vein, the Singapore Deputy Prime Minister Lee Hsien Loong argued that 'we have to participate in the international effort against terrorism because it is our responsibility as an international citizen. This is something all countries have to do together.'[5] Singapore made yet its clearest stance on the issue when its Foreign Minister, Professor S. Jayakumar, argued in a speech during the Ministerial Meeting on Counter-Terrorism at the United Nations Security Council that:

> Countering the threat of terrorism is clearly and rightly now a central global priority. The perpetrators of these horrendous crimes must not go unpunished. They must be brought to justice to deter others from contemplating similar horrific crimes.

> Singapore stands with the international community in this campaign against terrorism. This is not a fight against any religion. It is not a fight against the people of Afghanistan. It is a fight against the forces of violence, intolerance and fanaticism. It is a fight for civilization and a fight that we must win.
>
> We must grid ourselves for a long effort. The threats will come in many different forms. Some will be more virulent than others, some waxing while others wane. And, like disease, even as one source of terrorism is eradicated, others will spring up or mutate. Only a determined, united, comprehensive and sustained global strategy will enable the international community to contain these malignant forces.[6]

That there would be problems and challenges from the international dimension of the management of the post-11 September incident was something that did not miss the Singapore strategic radar. As argued by Lee Hsien Loong:

> . . . the US has to form a broad coalition, so that it's not just America against the Taliban—or worse, America against the Muslim countries—but many nations, non-Muslim and Muslim, in an international coalition against terrorism. If they can do that, then our position in Singapore is easier. But still, our problem won't completely disappear. In the Gulf War, Saudi Arabia, Egypt and many other Arab countries joined the allied forces against Iraq. Yet, the ground sentiments in these Muslim countries were strongly against the US, and against their own governments. This time, Pakistan's President Musharraf is in a very tough position. He declared that Pakistan supports the fight against terrorism but the ulamas and the crowds in the streets strongly sympathize with the Taliban and Osama bin Laden. These are trends that we have to be aware of, and try to guard against in Singapore.[7]

That these observations were sanguine and not off the mark were to be proven by events later, especially in the discovery of terrorist cells in the South-East Asian region, including Singapore that were networking with the Al-Qaeda, especially in Afghanistan.

Regional

Testifying to the increasingly globalized world, what transpired in New York and Washington on 11 September has had ramifications far and wide, and one region that directly felt its repercussions was South-East Asia. The region has always been somewhat plugged to the world strategically, politically and economically since 1945, and had never really escaped the consequences of whatever 'order' that dominated the world. This was equally true as far as 11 September was concerned, only this time its impact was negative. With Washington blaming Osama bin Laden and the Al-Qaeda network for the terrorist attack, and declaring war on all those who supported and harboured such terrorists, particularly the Taliban regime in Afghanistan, the US's anti-terrorist war eventually reached South-East Asia, mainly due to the links that were alleged to have existed between various terrorist groups in the region and those targeted by the US.

In this connection, particular attention was paid to Islamic terrorists that were alleged to be operating in Malaysia, Indonesia, and Philippines and eventually with a network discovered in Singapore in December 2001. The problem and challenge for Singapore was not simply managing its ties with its essentially Muslim neighbours (particularly, Malaysia and Indonesia) but also on the management of the new security threat of international terrorism that had networks in the region. While the Philippines and Malaysian governments were active in 'flushing' out these 'terrorists', the somewhat lackadaisical approach of Jakarta led to the worsening of ties, especially following the comments of Senior Minister Lee Kuan Yew that the Indonesian government was not doing enough to manage the terrorist threat.

Singapore's concern with the rise of Islamic militancy in the South-East Asian region was evident even before the 11 September incident due to its experience with this security threat in the past. This included, among others, the arrests made in 1987 of an Islamic spiritual group that was preparing for racial clashes on the anniversary of the 13 May 1969 riots in Malaysia.[8] Interestingly, exactly one week before the 11 September incident, during his visit to Malaysia, Senior Minister Lee Kuan Yew expressed concern about the rise of Islamic militancy in Malaysia, especially the threat posed by the Kumpulan Mujahideen Malaysia (KMM) or the Malaysian Mujahideen Group, essentially Malaysians that had supported the Mujahideen war against the Soviets in Afghanistan and later, continued to maintain ties with the Taliban regime. The KMM was alleged to be closely associated with the Al-Qaeda and to have a region-wide network in South-East Asia, aimed at creating a 'mega Islamic state' in the region. According to the Malaysian Defence Minister, Najib Razak, Lee Kuan Yew expressed concern about the

KMM activities because 'it will not only affect Malaysia but also Singapore'.[9]

Singapore's Deputy Prime Minister Lee Hsien Loong later argued that 'the Malaysian Government is very worried about the KMM whose members have trained in Afghanistan. These are facts which we have to take note off.'[10] He later elaborated his concern in the following terms:

> . . . that there are terrorist groups also in South-East Asia. For example, in the southern Philippines, there's the Abu Sayyaf and that's been traced back to a brother-in-law of Osama bin Laden who set it up and they are funding things and training groups. In Indonesia, there are also groups linked back to Osama and there are groups like the Lashkar Jihad which are fighting battles in the Malukus. And they are not just Indonesians fighting but Muslim extremists from other parts of the world who have come to Indonesia to join in the fight against Christians in the Malukus. In Malaysia, the government is very worried. They have this KMM, a group of people who have been trained in Afghanistan and come back to Malaysia.[11]

National

Traditionally, the Singapore government had always been wary of security threats from within (essentially communism and communalism) and without (largely, its neighbours).[12] Furthermore, it also had various experiences of terrorism in the past, including: the terrorist challenge posed by the Communist Party of Malaya, with 22 incidents of arsons and 11 bomb attacks alone between 1968 and 1974; the January 1974 'Laju Incident' involving terrorists from the Party of the Liberation of Palestine and Japanese Red Army; and the hijacking of a Vietnamese, Malaysian and Singaporean airline in October 1977, December 1977 and March 1991 respectively. Initially, the Singapore government was rather optimistic that there were no similar home-grown terrorist networks, with Lee Hsien Loong arguing that 'we are quite careful' even though he did qualify that the 'Americans didn't know they had these terrorists in America, either'.[13]

However, in December 2001, the government announced the arrest of a clandestine group of 13 Singaporeans under the Internal Security Act that had links with regional and international terrorists, and who were planning to bomb Western, especially American commercial and military targets in Singapore. All those arrested were believed to be members of Jemaah Islamiyah (JI). Eight of those arrested had received military training in Al-Qaeda camps in Afghanistan. Those arrested were described as 'foot soldiers' with the masterminds operating from abroad.[14] That the terrorists' threat to Singapore was real was further reinforced when the Singapore Prime Minister revealed on 5 April 2002 that five other members of the JI planned—a month after the arrest of 13 suspected terrorists—to hijack a plane and crash it into Changi International Airport in Singapore.[15]

This brought 11 September right onto the doorsteps of Singapore, making the Republic a part of the ongoing 'terrorist war', on the frontline, so to speak. The fact that this has had a religious dimension, with all those arrested being Muslims, merely complicated the problem, leading Prime Minister Goh Chok Tong to express concern about the future of inter-ethnic ties in the city-state: 'There is a global war against terrorism. This is not a war against Islam but events have shown that there can be repercussions for Muslim societies in particular. It will affect us if we do not strengthen our social cohesion. We have to consolidate our solidarity and create a more secure Singapore.'[16] How this problem and challenge will be managed remains to be seen: what is clear, however, is the fact that the 11 September incident had directly impinged upon Singapore's security at different levels and if anything, the Republic's sense of insecurity has been further aggravated. Increasingly, Singapore leaders have now been arguing that in addition to the economic slow-down, the threat posed by terrorism and its impact on inter-ethnic harmony has become the primary security concern of the Republic at present.

SINGAPORE, THE REGION AND SECURITY POLICIES IN THE POST-11 SEPTEMBER PERIOD

Nationally

- Used the Internal Security Act to nab 13 suspected terrorists belonging to the cell that called itself Jemaah Islamiah.
- Outlined a new homeland security framework to enhance co-operation between the Defence and Home Affairs ministries, under the purview of the Security Policy Review Committee. A 'special joint exercise' between the two ministries was organized in late January 2002, involving among others, the evacuation of

casualties in a chemical plant that had been sabotaged and decontaminating fire-fighters who had come into contact with chemicals as well as disposal of bombs.

- Emphasis on inter-ethnic harmony and peace through various mechanisms including the establishment of Inter-Racial Harmony Circles throughout the country.
- Establish a National Security Secretariat to strengthen coordination between all security agencies.[17]
- Passed the UN Act forbidding Singaporeans and foreigners in the Republic from assisting terrorists financially or otherwise, thereby criminalizing such acts.
- Signed the International Convention for the Suppression of the Financing of Terrorism.
- Expand budget for intelligence and counter-terrorism activities.
- Strengthen the Suspicious Transactions Reporting Office in order to stop money laundering activities that might involve international terrorism.

Regionally and globally

- Endorse United Nations counter-terrorism measures that have been passed by the Security Council since the 11 September incident.
- Support and endorse American anti-terrorist policies worldwide and in the region.
- Undertake closer intelligence cooperation with its ASEAN partners, best evident in the 'informal' meeting of the military intelligence chiefs in Kuala Lumpur in late January 2002.
- Provide intelligence and information to neighbours, among others, that led to the arrest of the alleged Indonesian bomb maker in the Philippines, Fathur Rohman Ghozi.

Possible Singapore–India Security Cooperation Post-9/11

There has been growing security cooperation between Singapore and India in the last decade or so, especially in the maritime area. The MOU between the two navies is testimony of this. Personnel of the Singapore Armed Forces also have a long history of training in various military academies in India. The Singapore Navy was particularly grateful for the assistance provided in submarine and anti-submarine warfare in the 1990s. In this connection, India's naval expansion and its policing of the waters in the Indian Ocean region, including in the Straits of Malacca region, has been deemed important in maintaining a 'balanced' presence in the vital waterways of the world through which passes much of the oil and merchant traffic of East Asia.

In the post-11 September era, India's experience in counter-terrorism, especially in a multi-cultural and multi-religious setting would be particularly useful for Singapore. As counter-terrorism in the post-11 September era has to be particularly sensitive to the Muslim population, it would be extremely useful to learn various lessons on how this had been undertaken in India. At the same time, with the growing role of India in countering terrorism internationally, India's role in assisting a US-led coalition in policing the waters around South-East Asia, especially in the Straits of Malacca, is likely to grow in importance and this would be useful in enhancing confidence-building security measures between India and the ASEAN region. This is where Singapore can play a useful bridging role, as it did in assisting India's membership in the ASEAN Regional Forum. In short, despite the growing concern with the threat of terrorism there is at the same time a growing window of opportunity for cooperation between the two countries in eradicating this scourge.

CONCLUSION

Even though Singapore has been described as a 'little dot', the power it has been able to bring to bear on regional and international politics far outweighs its size. As such, observers are fond of describing Singapore as a 'boxer' that punches 'above its weight'. This is most vividly evident in its foreign policy, largely determined by strategic, political and economic realities and more important, the will to survive and thrive in a largely unstable and uncertain region. Its continued commitment to ASEAN remains one of the central planks of its outlook and to that extent, ASEAN's importance and relevance will remain central to the foreign policy of this smallest South-East Asian state. At the same time, 11 September has demonstrated that there are threats that will emerge from time to time, and there are many security-related aspects that are beyond its control. Therein is located the tragedy and uncertainty of being a small, successful, essentially Chinese 'island' in a 'Malay Sea'.

NOTES

1. For example, see Andrew Tan, *Problems and Issues in Malaysia-Singapore Relation* (Canberra, Strategic and Defence Studies Centre, Australian National University, 1997), Working Paper No. 314, pp. 1–30; Andrew Tan, *Intra-ASEAN Tensions* (London: The Royal Institute of International Affairs, 2000), Discussion Paper No. 84, pp. 1–59.
2. For a better discussion of these, see Bilveer Singh, *The Vulnerability of Small States Revisited: A Study of Singapore's Post-Cold War Foreign Policy* (Jogjakarta: Gadjah Mada University Press, 1999), pp. 11–36; Michael Leifer, *Singapore's Foreign Policy: Coping with Vulnerability* (London: Routledge, 2000), pp. 27–42; Tim Huxley, *Defending the Lion City: The Armed Forces of Singapore* (Crows Nest, NSW, Australia: Allen and Unwin, 2000), pp. 24–72.
3. For a further discussion of this, see Bilveer Singh, op. cit., pp. 63–175.
4. See transcript of interview with DPM B.G. Lee Hsien Loong by Hwee Goh, Channel News Asia on 28 September 2001 (Singapore Government Press Release, Media Division, Ministry of Information and the Arts).
5. Cited in *The Straits Times*, 23 September 2001.
6. See Statement by Prof. S. Jayakumar, Minister for Foreign Affairs at the United Nations Security Council Ministerial Meeting on 12 November 2001 (Singapore Government Press Release, Media Division, Ministry of Information and the Arts).
7. Cited in *The Straits Times*, 23 September 2001.
8. See 'Not Crazy: That's why JI group's threat is real and scary', *Today,* 18 February 2002.
9. Cited in *Business Times* (Singapore), 4 September 2001.
10. See *The Straits Times*, 23 September 2001.
11. See Transcript of Interview with DPM B.G. Lee Hsien Loong by Hwee Goh, Channel News Asia on 28 September 2001.
12. See Bilveer Singh, 'Singapore: Management of its Security Problems', *Asia Pacific Community*, Summer 1985, no. 29, pp. 77–96; and Bilveer Singh, 'A Small State's Quest for Security: Operationalising Deterrence in Singapore's Strategic Thinking', in Ban Kah Choon, Anne Pakir and Tong Chee Kiong (eds.), *Imagining Singapore* (Singapore: Times Academic Press, 1992), pp. 97–131.
13. See *The Straits Times*, 23 September 2001.
14. According to investigations, a group of 20 people, organized in 4 cells, were planning to set off 7 simultaneous explosions in Singapore. The Singapore group had already obtained access to 4 tonnes of ammonia nitrate that was stored in Muar, Johor in Malaysia and had been given money to buy an additional 17 tonnes of chemical and 7 trucks. The trucks were each to contain 3 tonnes of nitrate and to be used as bombs, creating 7 simultaneous explosions. See *The Straits Times*, 10 February 2002.
15. The alleged hijacking was supposed to be led by Mas Selamat Kastari. However, before they could be arrested, they are believed to have fled to

Malaysia, following which, they are believed to have gone into Thailand and from there, to Medan in Indonesia via Langkawi (Malaysia). Their whereabouts have been unknown since then. For details, see 'PM reveals plans to crash jet into Changi', ibid., 6 April 2002 and 'Militants fled to Medan via Malaysia', ibid., 7 April 2002.

16. See *Business Times* (Singapore), 1 January 2002.
17. According to Dr Tony Tan, the Defence Minister, this was needed as 'Singapore was facing a new type of international terrorism, which was strategic in outlook, and much more dangerous and sustained than the one-off terrorist attacks carried out in the past by disparate groups'. It is not possible for us to deal with these new threats with the same type of structure and capabilities we had in the past'. Cited in *The Straits Times*, 7 January 2002.

Yong Mun Cheong

Moulding Public Perceptions in Singapore about the Indian Ocean

The central question to be addressed in this paper can be briefly phrased as follows: How did the Singapore government or other agencies attempt to 'prepare the ground' so that the public could be made aware of the international events unfolding around them, and, therefore, more conscious of how international relations can affect them individually, especially in relation to those international developments taking place in the Indian Ocean region?

It must not be assumed that the public in Singapore was naturally inclined to regard international affairs, international developments and international relations as areas of concern. No doubt the literacy rate had always been high in Singapore, and, therefore, the Singapore public would have been expected to keep abreast of international relations through newspapers and the media. No doubt too the fact that Singapore had always been a trading community, and as such it was compelled by force of circumstances to be ever cognizant of what was going on in the rest of the world. Awareness of international relations was almost a sine qua non of good business, and an essential ingredient for any trading venture. Even in a place like Singapore, it was necessary to prepare the ground. How was this done?

THE CONTRIBUTIONS OF S. RAJARATNAM

The major actors in this exercise were of course personnel within the Singapore government. In this regard, special mention must be made of the role of the former Foreign Minister, S. Rajaratnam. Beginning in the 1970s, and possibly even earlier, he embarked on an indefatigable exercise to educate the Singapore public about the international dangers lurking around, and how these dangers should be addressed. He gave talks on many occasions. He lectured. He spoke at seminars and conferences. On every occasion, he alerted the Singapore public to world developments that would impact on Singapore.

As background, Rajaratnam began his career as a journalist. He was a founder member of the People's Action Party (PAP). In 1959, with the electoral victory of the PAP, he was appointed Minister of Culture. In that capacity, he played the role of party ideologue, a position carved out for him, given his superior gift of language, his skill at building arguments, and his ability at developing ideas. When Singapore became independent in 1965, Rajaratnam was the obvious choice as foreign minister. He held this appointment till 1980. Thereafter, he was still active in foreign affairs, making forays into issues of international relations.

This part of the essay will focus on Rajaratnam's thoughts related to the Indian Ocean, but will not be confined to the Indian Ocean because it is not possible to conceive of the Indian Ocean without reference to the rest of the world. The Indian Ocean did not dominate the radar screen of the Singapore public, and its share of that radar screen only made sense in relation to the other areas of concern in international relations.

What was the Singapore public? It was any segment of Singapore society that was prepared to listen to S. Rajaratnam's domain specialization, namely, foreign affairs. Thus, S. Rajaratnam did not confine himself to discussing international relations with only international relations specialists. He made forays into the world of school students, members of karate associations, and even professionals in the society of gynaecologists and obstetricians. No group was too unfamiliar or so unimportant to discuss matters related to foreign affairs, and drive their attention to international developments in the Indian Ocean, and elsewhere.

He spoke in a language that was simple and easily understood. Concepts were explained in everyday terms. Many of these speeches and addresses were delivered during the 1970s–80s. The 1970s–80s were a critical period when the possibility of big-power conflict in the Indian Ocean loomed large. The period was marked by competition and rivalry for influence between the Soviet Union and the United States. There was a real danger that in this contest for influence, dominance and control, minuscule states like Singapore would see their interests sacrificed, ignored, and trampled upon. It was, therefore, important for its government to speak up, and for its public to be conscious of all these international developments taking place.

Rajaratnam had his work cut out for him. During the 1970s and 1980s, Singapore had just become newly independent. Survival was not to be assumed, and one of the first tasks of any foreign minister was to demonstrate that Singapore, despite the small size and the lack of resources, could survive. Then it was necessary to show that even small states had national interests that must be respected by other powers—big and small. This implied that Singapore must be able to conduct international relations with bigger states located in the Indian Ocean and elsewhere. Finally, the world of international relations had to be explained in everyday language such that the public in Singapore understood the dangers that confronted small states like Singapore.

How then did Rajaratnam prepare the ground? Although he did not say it, I thought Rajaratnam was almost behaving like a university teacher explaining basic concepts in a simple way to novice students who had just sauntered into a lecture hall, sleepy, uninterested, and overwhelmed. This was no mean feat. Even today, the average person in Singapore is hardly interested in international relations. Parochialism was and is the order of the day. Even discussions in Parliament did not often relate to international affairs. Perhaps the affairs of ASEAN may kindle some interest. And for the respective ethnic groups, the affairs of China, India or Malaysia may arouse some interest.

The following are samples of what I call the Rajaratnam approach to international relations.

The discussion will focus on two components: (1) the *message* or messages that Rajaratnam tried to convey to the public and (2) the *metaphors* he used to frame those messages. Both the message and the metaphor will be discussed together.

We start with a speech (of 1972) on the Indian Ocean. The context was the early 1970s. What was taking place there? Rajaratnam did not claim that he knew, and when ignorance abounded, it was perfectly normal and easily understood that people naturally looked for signposts to guide them. The image was that of a person (the persona of Singapore) gazing at a multiplicity of signposts hung up on a pole, each pointing in a different direction. This image was nothing extraordinary. Everyone would have seen drawings of people staring at signposts, trying to figure which way to go. In this image, one signpost would be labelled one destination, and another signpost would bear the label of another destination. For the signposts in the speech by Rajaratnam, there was only one problem. There were many signposts and they were all blank. He had no idea where the signposts were pointed at, and like all signposts, only one could be correct, i.e. pointed in the right direction. Singapore had arrived at the Indian Ocean but now had to negotiate a set of crossroads. It was like the crossroads of history, but this was the version of the Russian roulette. All the chambers were loaded, except one. The odds against picking the right chamber were considerable. According to Rajaratnam, that was why nations had halted at crossroads, and when they resumed their journey, the toll had been heavy.

The first proposition, therefore, was to stop playing Russian roulette, i.e. stop gambling with international relations. Russian roulette was a superficial and dangerous approach to international relations in the Indian Ocean. International relations should not be played like a game of dice. History was on the side of those leaders who submitted themselves to rationality and those who acknowledged realities. People should take calculated risks, but these risks were different from the risks taken when gambling. Rajaratnam argued that people should fill their own signposts. Fill them correctly, and the journey forward would be a safe one. Fill them wrong, and nations get lost and may even disappear forever. He then proceeded to fill up the signposts for the Indian Ocean.

On oceans in general, Rajaratnam argued in 1972 that there were only two nations with the technological and economic resources to enter the contest for sea power. The outlay of money, technology and organization was tremendous. This was because some five-sixths of the globe's surface is sea. A vast network of ships, ports, aircraft carriers, submarines were required for the exercise of global power over oceans. It was only recently that the United States and the then Soviet Union had discovered the importance of sea power. Rajaratnam predicted that the Indian Ocean was going to be the most important arena of contest. This situation had developed as a result of the British withdrawal east of Suez in 1968. As he put it, the Indian Ocean was put up for auction. The littoral states were not able to control the Indian Ocean, either singly or even collectively. To control the oceans, naval power was needed. This was beyond the reach of the littoral states, unlike say the control of land.

The interest in the Indian Ocean was not only strategic. It was also commercial. Rajaratnam went on to discuss the Soviet merchant fleet and the Soviet fishing fleet. The Indian Ocean was the only place where the Soviet fleets from the Atlantic, Mediterranean and the Pacific could meet. The most prudent solution, according to Rajaratnam, was to work towards a balance of power that will allow small nations to share in the world's oceans.

Other messages were less directly related to the Indian Ocean but nevertheless relevant. Rajaratnam pressed for the development of what he called 'small nation' diplomacy or 'S N diplomacy' (1972), particularly relevant for Singapore in the zone of the Indian Ocean. S N diplomacy was a series of studies to enable small nations to cope with the practical problems of diplomacy. S N diplomacy was not about how small nations could avoid being swallowed up by big powers. This danger he regarded as least likely. Rather, big powers harassed small nations by exploiting conflicts and rivalries between small nations. S N diplomacy was about small nations of Asia fashioning diplomacy to avoid small wars and proxy wars.

In this same vein, Rajaratnam described small nations as Davids in a world of Goliaths (1972). Applying the metaphor to Singapore, he asked in what way could Singapore maximize its chances of survival in a world with many great powers? How can a couple of million people meet military threats? How can a couple of million people ensure prosperity and internal peace? An immediate measure was to abandon what he described in the metaphor of 'midget neurosis'. The abandonment of midget neurosis would enable Singapore to stand shoulder to shoulder in a world of Goliaths—whether in the Indian Ocean or elsewhere.

Another metaphor that Rajaratnam advanced was the global city (1972), and Singapore was fast becoming one. As he explained, the global city was a new form of human organization and settlement, a child of modern technology, a city made inevitable by electronic communication, giant tankers and modern economic and industrial organization. With regards to the Indian Ocean, the global city was important because the Indian Ocean, like other oceans, was its hinterland. Singapore had become interdependent within a rapidly expanding global economic system and that included the Indian Ocean.

In connection with the Straits of Malacca, Rajaratnam argued for the unimpeded passage of all ships of all nations through the seas. In this way, the world could avoid a dangerous scramble for the carving up of the oceans. Hitherto, most conflicts known to mankind were related to the division of land and rectification of land frontiers. Now that the world's land mass had already been claimed and divided up, Rajaratnam argued that there could well be a scramble for the oceans, including the Indian Ocean. If the scramble did take place, then the small nations like Singapore would surely be the losers.

In 1973, at the United Nations, Rajaratnam warned about the impending dangers of a scramble for the control of the oceans and the seas. Without naming any body of waters, Rajaratnam argued that the world had entered the era of ocean politics and ocean economics.

The scramble for the seas was not a figment of the imagination. By the 1980s, the Soviet navy was roaming the Seven Seas, and the navy had established itself in strategic areas around the Indian Ocean. During the invasion and occupation of Afghanistan, the Soviets could fan out into Pakistan, Iran and eventually into the Gulf States. Soon, it would be the turn of the Indian Ocean. Rajaratnam was chiefly concerned with the success of Soviet power despite all odds. As late as 1981, he expressed this concern, saying that within a short space of thirty years, Soviet power was able to expand from East Berlin to the Kurile Islands, with forward bases in the Caribbean, the Red Sea, South-East Asia, and West Asia. As skilled with words as he was, Rajaratnam coined a term to describe Soviet tentacles extending over the world. He called them the 'Brezhnev scenario'. To Brezhnev, détente was an ideological weapon to realize the dominance of Communism over Capitalism. Thus, Communists would confront this Capitalism one day, not on the basis of accords, but from a superior economic and military position.

To explain the increasing influence of the Soviet Union, and especially its navy in the blue waters of Asia, Rajaratnam coined the metaphor of the 'arrogance of morality' (1980). This arrogance of morality was about the Western liberals who denigrated and humiliated those Asian nations with poor human rights records.

Rajaratnam argued that Western liberals needed to understand that this stress on morality contributed to the reluctance of the United States to support Asian regimes to stand up against the spread of Soviet influence.

THE CONTRIBUTIONS OF G.G. THOMSON

The credit for preparing the ground cannot be given only to Rajaratnam. Contemporary with Rajaratnam was another person called the late G.G. Thomson whose discussions on the Indian Ocean and the seas in general aroused the consciousness of the Singapore public. G.G. Thomson was certainly less well known than Rajaratnam. The former was a civil servant during the colonial period. When the British devolved self-government to Singapore, Thomson was one of those expatriate civil servants who decided to serve the new local administration. He later was appointed Director of the Political Studies Centre, a training institution for civil servants to strengthen their ideological awareness of the task they had been entrusted to do. Upon his retirement, G.G. Thomson kept himself busy attending academic conferences, and contributed several extensive pieces on maritime issues that concerned Singapore. He was well known for alerting the Singapore public to the strategic importance of the Straits of Malacca as well as the Law of the Sea issues.

Unlike Rajaratnam, his public assertions were academic, and not popular in the sense that they did not appeal to the general public. Also unlike Rajaratnam, his public statements were not metaphorical in the sense that it was not his style to use metaphors that would capture the essence of what he wanted to say and at the same time capture the attention of the public by their uniqueness, as did Rajaratnam. What G.G. Thomson did was to provide history lessons based on his observations of the Indian Ocean.

In terms of content, G.G. Thomson and Rajaratnam wrote and spoke about the 1970s, and both devoted considerable attention to maritime issues.

Like Rajaratnam, G.G. Thomson viewed the Russians as a threat that was becoming very powerful in the Indian Ocean. He dated the maritime interest of Russia from 1968, and this maritime interest was a result of its great power strategic role, its economic interests, and not really a result to spread the Leninist revolution. The desire to surround China from the seas also contributed to this maritime interest. By mid-1969, Russia had entered the Malaysian rubber market in a big way. In Sihanouk's Cambodia, Russia was deeply engaged in programmes of economic development. Russian interests in the Indian Ocean were also due to the need to recover one of its Sputniks. Russian naval ships were sent into the Indian Ocean, and that started their visiting the ports of Africa and India. It was not Russian policy to establish naval bases but to ensure that the countries abutting the Indian Ocean developed facilities that the Russians could use and were allowed to use. Generally, the Indian Ocean was important for Russia if only to deny the Americans the opportunity to use the ocean.

Thomson tried to demonstrate the importance of the seas to South-East Asia and the Singapore public. He continually stressed that 70 per cent of South-East Asia consisted of water; 60 per cent of its people lived on islands. All the capitals were accessible from the sea, except Vientiane. The basic pattern of communication was the sea, and the sea provided wealth as well as the source of living.

G.G. Thomson also brought to attention several interesting facts about the seas, and although these facts no longer contain much interest now, they were novelties in the 1970s, and represented interpretations that had not been thought through before.

He debunked the myth that the land unites while the sea divides. In history, it was the sea that rendered ineffective the land barriers posed by the mountains and deserts. The ship enabled mankind to make more history than the horse or the camel. Therefore, oceanic thinking must balance the default mode of thinking, namely, continental thinking. Coming closer to Asia, G.G. Thomson debunked the second myth that because Asia was the world's largest land-mass, the sea was less important. Asia was the only continent with two oceans (the Indian and Pacific Oceans). There were in fact three Asias, one of the land, and two of the oceans. Of the three components, the dominant parts of Asia looked seawards to the Indian Ocean and the Pacific Ocean, rather than landwards.

G.G. Thomson highlighted a number of negatives about the Indian Ocean. Significantly, there was no pacemaker, like that of Japan in the Pacific Ocean. G.G. Thomson noted that no state in the Indian Ocean was compulsively oceanic in economic and strategic outlook. Neither India nor Indonesia fulfilled the role that Japan played in the Pacific. The Indian Ocean also did not have the same spread of islands and atolls that served as stepping-stones of commerce or strategy. While navigational conditions were helpful, there were only a few good ports. This absence of good ports was partly a result of the limited needs of imperial power and international transit. The British were also able to keep out rival port and power builders from the Indian Ocean. And when they withdrew from Asia, the withdrawal was generally regarded as a naval withdrawal, not an air or military withdrawal.

Upon British withdrawal, G.G. Thomson noted the development of a vacuum. He had interesting comments on the Indian reaction to what was happening in the Indian Ocean then. India viewed British power as imperial and illegitimate. The existence of naval power negated and did not contribute to peace. In 1970, the Indian Ministry of External Affairs thought that the British withdrawal would not create any more of a power vacuum than the liquidation of the British Empire had created. What mattered to the countries of the Indian Ocean was the need to build their economies to resist aggression. It was not necessary to plant a few ships here and there to make it possible for the Indians to say they had a presence.

G.G. Thomson was less sanguine. His mission was to draw the attention of the Singapore public to the importance of the Indian Ocean, in terms of strategy, commerce and mere proximity. In his view, India could be threatened from the sea. If India's threats were landward, it was only from the sea that assistance could arrive. The problem was not India. It was South-East Asia that showed scant interest in the Indian Ocean. The problems of South-East Asia were less likely to debouch on to the Indian Ocean, and that accounted for the lack of interest. This had to be addressed, and it was the mission of G.G. Thomson to start a public discussion in Singapore and elsewhere.

CONCLUSION

Since the days of Rajaratnam and Thomson, circumstances have changed. Sometimes one wonders what is the relevance of these earlier pronouncements about the Indian Ocean. It will be useful to attempt a survey of how the different circumstances have affected the way the Indian Ocean region is viewed from the Singapore angle.

For one, with the end of the Cold War, the agenda is no longer characterized by Cold War rivalry. The emergence of the USA as the single world power meant that the great ideological division between Communism and Capitalism had faded, and the clients in each division have gone their own way. There is potential for independent agendas. What these will be is not clear but such independent agendas leave much room for manoeuvre for the Indian Ocean.

There is now less justification for great power intervention in the internal affairs of the states of the Indian Ocean region unless there is a perceived threat to the interests of the USA, as in the Iraq-Kuwait war and in the Afghanistan war against the Taliban.

Perhaps because of the rise of different types of technologies, there are fewer people working the oceans as fishermen, sailors or travellers. The exchange of culture and religion via the Indian Ocean, using the ocean as a highway, no longer holds true. In fact, oceans no longer boast the role of transmitting culture or religion. That claim is best left to cyberspace, celluloid or print.

Oceans—and the Indian Ocean is not an exception—now gain ecological significance. Oceans are viewed in terms of rising sea levels due to global warming. Oceans are a major source of desalinated water even as the technology to purify seawaters improves. Oceans continue to be a major source of food. There is heightened consciousness of oceans as ecologically relevant for marine life. Measures are taken to regulate the fishing industry so that overfishing does not occur.

On the whole, the interest in oceans has declined, notwithstanding the crusading speeches and writings of Rajaratnam and company. The development of statehood and nation-states turned the people along the Indian Ocean rim inwards rather than seawards. Nation-states were introduced by the Western colonial authorities in most cases, and such states invariably centred on citizenship, loyalty towards a given landed territory (never a maritime area), delivery of services from a central authority located somewhere inland.

If there is any interest in oceans, two areas can be identified, one historical and the other contemporary.

There is still scholarly interest of a historical kind in oceans. One area of research that cries out for more attention is the considerable cultural/religious exchange through the Muslim pilgrimage. In the nineteenth and early twentieth centuries, many believers undertook the arduous journey from South-East Asia (especially the Dutch East Indies) to the Middle East. There were major transit points along the Indian Ocean shores that were important in this religious journey. Would-be pilgrims left Batavia or Kuala Lumpur for Singapore before proceeding further. In Singapore, they caught the KPM ship that brought them to Jeddah, stopping at ports along the Indian Ocean. The religious and cultural experiences along the Indian Ocean crossing require further investigation. These experiences are less pronounced today as pilgrims tend to fly to their destinations.

The contemporary interest in the Indian Ocean is now encapsulated as part of the programme of regionalization. In addition to investing in China, entrepreneurs in Singapore are urged to consider opportunities in South Asia. The same impetus, incentives and encouragement that apply to China now also applies to South Asia. How the ground is prepared to make the public more aware of these opportunities is another chapter in this piece of research.

REFERENCES

Chee, Chan Heng and Obaid ul Haq (eds.), *The Prophetic & the Political: Selected Speeches & Writings of S. Rajaratnam*, Singapore: Graham Brash, and New York: St Martins Press, 1987.

McPherson, Kenneth, *The Indian Ocean: A History of People and the Sea*, Delhi: Oxford University Press, 1993.

Shaw, K.E. and George G. Thomson, *The Straits of Malacca: in relation to the problems of the Indian and Pacific Oceans*, Singapore: University Education Press, 1973.

Singapore Government Press Statement, Ministry of Culture, 1972–80.

Singh, Jasjit (ed.), *Bridges across the Indian Ocean*, New Delhi: Institute for Defence Studies and Analysis, 1997.

Paramjit S. Sahai

Cultural Diplomacy: India in Singapore

> *I do not want my house to be walled and my windows to be stuffed. I want the culture of all lands to be blown about my house as freely as possible, but I refuse to be blown off my feet by any one of them.*
>
> MAHATMA GANDHI

I start with the inimitable and profound words of Mahatma Gandhi as these are still relevant to any discussion on cultural matters. These are also topical, as Mahatma Gandhi as a brand name has become the subject of a recent controversy following the efforts of an American Company—CMG Worldwide—to acquire rights on the use of this name. Mahatma Gandhi beckons us to an important thought—his faith in an open space and an open mind to other cultures, but with a firm faith in one's own culture. This openness paves the way for promoting understanding between diverse cultures across the world at the present juncture when we are in the throes of a clash of civilizations.

When I decided to choose this topic, I did not realize its enormity and complexity. I thought that it would be a cakewalk, having practiced cultural diplomacy over the last thirty-seven years in my diplomatic career. It had become a part of daily life routine as one organized one or another cultural activity. Now I even find myself stumbling over the definition of 'Cultural Diplomacy'. I, therefore, plan to give a theoretical base to the topic, while I continue to examine the same at the practical level. I plan to divide my paper into a number of sub-heads for purposes of easier understanding for myself and hope that in the process I succeed in doing the same for the scholars and experts. I plan to deal with the topic under sub-heads such as, Culture; Indian Culture; Cultural

Diplomacy; India's Cultural Diplomacy at the Global Level; Policy Framework and Cultural Institutions; India's Cultural Links with the South-East Asian Countries; India's Cultural Diplomacy in Singapore; and finally coming up with suggestions which are relevant in promoting cultural links between India and South-East Asia, including Singapore.

CULTURE

To start with, it will be essential to understand what we mean by the term 'culture'. Culture includes art, music, dance, and drama and is a whole way of life; it is a *sanskriti* or a process of refinement. Culture concerns 'the entire gamut of human activity and achievement'.[1] In short, culture is a total social heritage acquired by man as a member of society. Culture is shared and has distinctive forms (patterns) and shapes of human behaviour. Its essence is the values embodied in the beliefs of people and the value orientation patterns become the essential features of culture.[2] It is the 'summation of material and creative resources of a people living within identifiable geographical frontiers'.[3] The culture of a nation finds its manifestation through language and art, philosophy and religion, education and science, films and newspapers, radio and television, social habits and customs, political institutions and economic organizations.

We are adopting this holistic definition of culture since UNESCO, at its 1982 Conference in Mexico, also adopted a similar one. It reads, 'Culture comprises the whole complex of distinctive spiritual, material, intellectual and emotional features that characterizes a society or social group. It includes not only the arts and letters, but also modes of life, the fundamental rights of the human being, value systems, traditions and beliefs.'[4]

Culture in the context of nation-states results in their acquiring a personality of their own. Each nation thus acquires a distinct personality and a national stereotype. At times such stereotypes are at variance with reality as it is the perceptions that matter. At other times, they are politically motivated to promote particular interests of the state. At times an effort is made to put across ideas which are in tune with different cultures. George Bush's war against terrorism is now described as 'Operation Freedom' in replacement of the original epithet 'Operation Justice', after it became known that under Islam only God can mete out justice. His recent reference to Iraq, Iran and North Korea, as 'an Axis of Evil' is also couched in cultural terms, even though it has led to some murmurs of protest among Europeans.

Lee Kuan Yew recently commented in his book on such cultural stereotypes when he said: 'The Tunku's simple belief was that "politics was for Malays and business for the Chinese". This might have been so in his father's time, but was not realistic in 1962.'[5] We hear of the Ugly American, the Russian Bear, the ASEAN (Association of South-East Asian Nations) Tigers, the Indian Elephant, the Hindu Rate of Growth. We all have not only heard but seen the working of the ASEAN Way, which is 'to talk things out and settle most problems by "Mushawara" (consultation) and "Muwafakat" (consensus)'.[6]

Culture is an integrated whole and is not merely a sum total of its parts. Culture, as a totality of ways of life of a people, includes, among others, the economy of a society. Cultural development, therefore, refers to 'development of all aspects of a Society's life'. Gunnar Myrdal's thesis in *Asian Drama* that traditional societies could not modernize without giving up their beliefs and values is no more valid. Culture constitutes a balancing and a driving force of development and an objective of development itself.[7] Culture is a living phenomenon and is dynamic and not static in nature. No culture is either rigid enough not to allow for change or docile enough to allow itself to be submerged. Interaction among different cultures, therefore, gives rise to acculturation.[8]

Culture identifies for us an 'entire people and eras in terms of the ways in which we think they see or saw the world. It helps us to place them vis-à-vis one another, usually with ourselves at the centre of the world and at the end of time. It is, in short, a way of organizing the world, its time and space.'[9]

INDIAN CULTURE

Two things immediately strike one about Indian culture—its pluralistic nature and its composite character. Indian culture is not seen in a segmented way either in terms of language, region, or religion. We do not hear of a Hindu or Muslim or Christian view of Indian culture nor do we hear of it being Assamese or Bengali, Punjabi or Tamil culture.

The former and late Indian Vice-President, Krishan Kant, has beautifully summed up Indian culture's pluralistic character in the following words:

> [The] Indian Constitution embodies the spirit of Indian Civilization, which visualizes the one in the many and the many in the one. India has always been a land of many religions, many ethnic strains and many languages. Acceptance of diversity or tolerance with us is more than what is usually connected by the concept of secularism. Mahatma Gandhi expressed the idea in the following words: 'There is in Hinduism room enough for Jesus, as there is for Mohammed, Zoroaster and Moses.' In the Indian concept unity represents truth, which is many faceted. This makes India 'a diversity in unity'. Vivekanand put this succinctly when he said that we not only 'tolerate' but 'accept' others' faiths. The national poet Subrahmanya Bharati, in his famous poem, sang that Mother India spoke in eighteen languages. It is the very essence of our culture and an inseparable part of our outlook.[10]

Asghar Ali Engineer, in an article 'Minorities: Many-splendoured Contributions', highlights the fact that 'no single community can claim the entire credit for the richness of its culture and traditions' and how it has inherited a 'composite culture'. He concludes: 'The strength of Indian democracy lies in its plurality. Historically we have a pluralist society and the more we recognize the role of pluralism in our country the better it will be for its future.'[11] Under Articles 25 to 30 of the Constitution of India, both religious as well as cultural and linguistic minorities are protected. Cultural pluralism and its protection were accepted as the duty of the king. His protection of *dharma* was not religion in the modern sense, for it enveloped the 'entire range of social obligations of which religious ritual was a part'.[12]

The four basic wheels of Indian culture are family; religion; arts, music and drama; and literature and philosophy. These all have remained functional and have been renewed by successive generations, giving 'continuity to India as a civilizational force'.[13]

CULTURAL DIPLOMACY

The importance and role of cultural diplomacy depends on the role 'culture' is expected to play in shaping international relations. Its role has been viewed differently at different times in different societies. In the olden times culture followed trade in some cases, like the Silk Route, while in other cases, trade followed culture, like the spread of Buddhism in South-East Asia. B.P. Singh considers culture as a third important factor in determining the status of a country in the community of nations. In the post-Cold War scenario, the economic strength of a country as measured in terms of its share in international trade has emerged as the preponderant factor, replacing military muscle as the most important factor in the global power game. It is 'the cultural strength of a country that gives it cohesiveness, endurance and a memory to carry the country forward as a civilization in the world'.[14]

Culture should take primacy over other factors as culture can help us in creating an appropriate climate or environment, which is conducive for developing relations among different countries. This need for understanding was clearly spelt out by the then Prime Minister Nehru in 1950 at the time of the inauguration of the Indian Council for Cultural Relations (ICCR). He said, 'Therefore it becomes essential that we must try to understand each other in the right way. The right way is important. That right approach, the friendly approach is important, because a friendly approach brings a friendly response.'[15] M.C. Chagla, as president of ICCR, in his inaugural address at a seminar organized by ICCR in 1966 on 'India and South-East Asia', had observed that 'Culture has greater influence over minds than science or technology or industrial growth and if there is that cultural bond that brings minds together, that is the more lasting bond than any other.'[16]

What Nehru said in 1950, Prime Minister P.V. Narasimha Rao put in his own words in 1994 while delivering the Singapore Lecture that Indian cultural heritage would survive

> . . . all onslaughts from outside, integrating healthy influences and also influencing external factors in the process. The information revolution should have, as its natural corollary, an enlightened understanding of our cultural affinities and differences. The more we know of each other, the better we understand each other. Geographical, linguistic and legal barriers must come down.[17]

Cultural diplomacy, therefore, would imply the use of the art of diplomacy in promoting culture, which if we consider as a way of life of a group of people would amount to projecting a particular group to another, resulting in creating awareness of one and another. Such awareness leads to interaction among various players—states and individuals. This could be achieved through organizations of mega events or through a series of cultural activities with which a particular nation-state is identified. It would thus result in our using the instrumentality of 'culture' in promoting a country's diplomatic interests in commercial, political and strategic fields.

Cultural diplomacy would, therefore, imply a two-pronged action—the vanguard action would be to 'create a cultural presence' and the rearguard would be to 'ensure how the other person or nation would recognize and understand the projecting nation'.[18] This would mean projecting the brand equity of a nation. Ambassador K.S. Rana dwells at length on Indian brand equity and states that the task of cultural diplomacy would be 'to produce understanding that goes beyond stereotyped images and to mould perceptions in a favourable way'.[19]

In practice, it would, however, be more preferable to project the correct image of a nation. In the case of India while projecting 'India Advantage' we should not shy away from recognizing 'India Disadvantage' as lasting relationship among nations can only be built up on the basis of credibility. Building up of a cultural image, therefore, becomes more difficult as it is an exercise in intangibles, resulting more from perceptions rather than reality.

INDIA'S CULTURAL DIPLOMACY AT THE GLOBAL LEVEL

India recognized the role and importance of cultural diplomacy even prior to becoming independent. It was at the Asian Relations Conference held in New Delhi in 1946 that it was resolved to set up the Indian Council for Cultural Relations for 'strengthening the ties of cultural cooperation and exchange between India and other Asian countries'. The mandate of ICCR was, however, expanded to cover all other countries at the behest of Indian leaders like Jawaharlal Nehru and Maulana Abul Kalam Azad.

ICCR, therefore, became the nodal agency involved with the promotion of Indian cultural links with the world. It was set up in April 1950 and its objectives are defined in the Memorandum of Association, which reads as follows:

- To establish, revive and strengthen cultural relations and mutual understanding between India and other countries.
- To promote cultural exchanges with other countries.
- To adopt all other measures as may be required to further its objectives.[20]

ICCR has, in fact, taken upon itself the 'twin task of promoting and interpreting abroad Indian culture in its widest sense as well as in establishing, reviving and strengthening cultural ties between India and other countries'.[21]

India's first Education Minister, Maulana Abul Kalam Azad, was the first to recognize both the role of the state and its limitations, which still form the broad contours of India's cultural policy. He said, 'In a democratic regime, the arts can derive their sustenance only from people and the State—as the organized manifestation of the people's will—must, therefore, undertake its maintenance and development as one of its first responsibilities.' Later the Haksar Committee recommended that more public funds would be 'invested in creating and maintaining a useful infrastructure for cultural activities rather than organizing cultural events'. The government is, therefore, expected to play a restrictive role and not to get involved in the execution of cultural programmes or activities.

POLICY FRAMEWORK AND CULTURAL INSTITUTIONS

In keeping with the above-mentioned broad policy, the government set about establishing a number of institutions, such as three national academies—Sangeet Natak Akademi (1953), Lalit Kala Akademi (1954) and Sahitya Akademi (1954)—as well as the National Museum (1954), the National School of Drama (1959) and the National Archives. Later other institutions such as the National Gallery of Modern Art and the Nehru Memorial Museum & Library were added. A new addition is Indira Gandhi National Centre for the Arts (IGNCA) which has succeeded in establishing dialogue among the sciences, technology, the humanities and the arts. A distinguishing feature has been the centre's 'multi-disciplinary and cross-cultural and multi-media exhibitions, seminars, and publications',[22] which are very important in creating interest among the new generation in the subtleties of culture.

India has adopted the instrumentality of bilateral cultural agreements in promoting cultural cooperation. While entering into these agreements, India has adopted a broader definition of culture, as these agreements cover all the fields of human activities such as education, science and technology, sports, arts and literature, archives and heritage, etc. India has until now signed cultural agreements with 112 countries. It may however be mentioned that cultural exchanges have taken place also with those countries with whom no such agreements exist, such as the USA, UK, etc., where direct institutional links have been developed or already exist.

Cultural agreements only provide a broad framework for co-operation. The implementation arrangement is worked out through an instrumentality called the Cultural Exchange Programme (CEP). CEP is always for a specific period, which may vary from one to three years, and it lists out the specific areas for cooperation and the implementation agencies thereof. There is always an element of reciprocity, as each programme has a sending body and a host. CEP is in the form of a letter of intent, as implementation is not binding in character, as it depends upon the implementing agencies and availability of funds. India at present has 78 CEPs with different countries. The implementation record varies from country to country and had been the highest with the erstwhile Socialist countries, which attached great importance to cultural linkages. A 50 per cent implementation of CEP would be a good track record.

ICCR has used three important instrumentalities—Chairs of Indian Studies, Cultural Centres and Festivals of India—in promoting cultural interests in the broader context. Other important activities include receiving distinguished visitors from abroad, receiving foreign students, holding seminars, and undertaking activities connected with the promotion of Indian art, music and dance. It also receives cultural troupes from foreign countries.

At present ICCR has 17 Visiting Professors and Chairs of Indian Studies abroad. Out of these, 11 are in Hindi,[23] 2 in Sanskrit (Bangkok and Paris), 1 in Tamil (Warsaw), 2 in Modern Indian History/South Asian Affairs and Civilization (Port of Spain, Osh in Kyrghystan), and in International Relations, Diplomacy and International Law (Tashkent).

There are 14 cultural centres abroad, which are currently run by ICCR. Out of these, 3 are in Europe (Moscow, London and Berlin), 3 in Americas (Georgetown, Paramaribo, Port of Spain), 4 in Africa (Cairo, Port Louis, Johannesburg and Durban) and 4 in Asia (Colombo, Tashkent, Almaty and Jakarta).

Festivals of India have been the latest entrant and the first such festival was organized in London in 1982. This concept owes its origin to the genius of Pupul Jayakar. Festivals of India were developed to project both traditional and modern India and to remove the stereotype of India as a fossilized monolith, a romantic and exotic land of maharajas, tigers, snake charmers, the Taj Mahal and, of course, grinding poverty.[24] ICCR organized festivals in 'countries which were considered important to us economically, politically and strategically'.[25] The success of this experiment would be more lasting if we are able to keep up the momentum of interest generated abroad by continuously organizing follow-up events. Otherwise, these would be lost in the sands of history, as Pupul Jayakar put it: 'To organize a festival is to float oil lamps in tiny boats on a river for an instant to illumine the ripples on the water and the rapt faces of those that participate in the launching; to set before the mirror of attention, times past and times present; and when the festival ends, to disappear like the boats, into the night.'[26]

I was personally involved in some of the activities connected with the Festival of India in USA during 1985–7 which was jointly launched by the late Prime Minister Rajiv Gandhi and the then President Ronald Reagan. The festival helped in launching India into the twenty-first century. The positive impact of the festival was noticed by the Parliamentary Standing Committee of the Ministry of External Affairs in its report submitted to the Lok Sabha in April 1997.

The magnitude and the range of cultural activities mounted by ICCR can be gauged by glancing through ICCR's latest Annual Report for the year 1999–2000. Under its Visitor's Programme it received 57 visitors/delegations from different parts of the world, while it sponsored and assisted the visit of 71 Indian scholars, intellectuals, academicians and artists to participate in seminars, symposia and international conferences abroad. The council sponsored the visit of 72 cultural groups to 61 countries, while it received 23 groups from abroad. The council organized four exhibitions in India, while it sent five exhibitions abroad. Under its scholarship programme, it offered 1,094 scholarships to students from 60 countries and the percentage utilization was 64 per cent. At present, the council is supporting 1,800 students from 75 countries. The council continued supporting the activities of its cultural centres and Chairs of Indian Studies abroad. It incurred an annual expenditure of Rs. 375 million during this year; out of this an amount of Rs. 42 million and Rs. 1 million was spent on incoming and outgoing visitors/delegations and seminars respectively. Expenditure on running of cultural centres amounted to Rs. 142 million, while Chairs of Indian Studies received a support of Rs. 20 million.

Diplomatic missions abroad play a vital role in planning and executing various items of cultural exchange. Their role is becoming increasingly difficult with the people losing interest in culture related activities in this age of consumerism. It needs a tremendous amount of energy and effort, and coordination with various organizations before any cultural event is mounted. Furthermore, the success would depend again in ensuring that there is an appropriate clientele willing to participate in this activity. A successfully organized event, however, is a satisfying experience and worth all the effort.

An evaluation of the role of the ICCR was undertaken by Parliament in 1996–7 and it finds mention in the second report of the Standing Committee on External Affairs.[27] The main thrust of the report was on ICCR being given 'real functional autonomy in pursuit of its objectives' as this would 'at the same time confer on it greater credibility'. It also talked about the 'need for continuous reorientation of the activities of the cultural centres abroad not only to meet the cultural thrust which ICCR is supposed to emphasize but also to improve India's image and further our own policy objectives'. It recognized the importance of the ICCR projecting 'a holistic image of a vibrant India'. It talked of involvement of the private sector and the need and desirability of more funds for cultural diplomacy. The report also stressed the need for assessing the utility of Chairs on Indian Studies 'in the context of contemporary needs and complaints' and recommended the need for 'setting up new Chairs with the emphasis on the study of contemporary India in selected target countries'. It wanted the ICCR to give added focus to activities other than the performing arts, so as to avoid being unwittingly identified in public perception 'as a kind of impresario organization'. This emphasis on the directional change of the activities of ICCR would be of interest to the participants as academic institutions now can look for additional support from ICCR in conducting seminars and other activities.

INDIA'S CULTURAL LINKS WITH SOUTH-EAST ASIA

A number of publications are available on India's historical and cultural links with South-East Asia. There is, however, paucity of material on India's present-day cultural links with these countries. The old ties did not automatically pave the way for strengthening our bilateral links in cultural and other areas. The sensitivities attached to the traditional Indian influence and the presence of a large number of persons of Indian origin (PIOs) made the newly independent governments circumspect in strengthening cultural bonds with India. The fact of 'a close cultural affinity then turns out to be some kind of hindrance rather than a help in forging new ties with a neighbouring country'. [28] Our differences on political and strategic issues in the 1970s and early 1980s also added to this low level of contacts.

There is a congruity of interest now and an Indian connection is seen in a positive light. The factors which have influenced this perception are as follows:

- A growing recognition of the need to understand the phenomenon of acculturation where the indigenous contribution of South-East Asian culture is presented in its proper perspective[29] and the need to see South-East Asia as 'a confluence area'.[30]
- Recognition that India has equally gained from the process as 'the footprints of ASEAN are to be seen in every aspect of India's ethos'.[31]
- Acceptance of India's cultural links in the present-day context, where we see a country like Malaysia promoting itself as 'Truly Asia' representing Indian, Chinese and Malay cultures. The government of Singapore is now taking steps to generate awareness among its people of their cultural roots in India and China.
- Prospects of increased economic and commercial links with India consequent to India's liberalized economic policies.
- Indian acceptance as ASEAN's Full Dialogue Partner (FDP) in 1996.

South-East Asia continues to remain a thrust area for India's cultural diplomacy. India signed a cultural agreement with Indonesia on 29 December 1995. This was followed by cultural agreements with the Philippines (06.09.69), Vietnam (18.12.76), Thailand (29.04.77), Malaysia (03.03.78), Laos (17.08.94) and Cambodia (31.01.96). A memorandum of understanding was signed with Singapore on 5 February 1993.

Cultural exchange programmes (CEPs) exist with Cambodia (2000–2), Indonesia (2001–3), Vietnam (2001–3) and Malaysia (2000–2). An executive programme exists with Singapore for the years 2000–2. CEPs with Indonesia, Laos, Cambodia, Vietnam and

Malaysia are of a broad nature, covering various fields under the sub-heads of education, health, culture and arts, youth affairs and sports and mass media. CEP with Vietnam is the most exhaustive one, while the executive programme with Singapore is restricted only to arts, archives and heritage.

A Chair of Indian Studies was set up at the Nanyang University in August 1970.[32] This Chair, however, has ceased to exist, as this university was merged with the Singapore University to form the National University of Singapore. Another Chair of Indian Studies was set up in 1971 in Indonesia,[33] while Chairs were established in 1972 in two universities in Thailand.[34] An Indo-Thai Buddhist institution was also established at Varanasi.[35]

A cultural centre at Jakarta was set up in 1988. The centre runs regular classes in *tabla*, *kathak* dance and *yoga*. Besides this, a teacher of Sanskrit and Hindi Studies was posted at the Udyana University, Bali, since 1 April 1999. The centre organizes cultural programmes, exhibitions, lectures, seminars and Hindi film shows. It also maintains a small library of books on Indian art and culture and an audio-visual library on Indian music, dance and Hindi films.

Over the years we have seen a number of specific recommendations emerge from a number of seminars and conferences organized by ICCR and IIC (India International Centre). It will be useful to have a look at these recommendations and see their connectivity with the present level of our links with the ASEAN countries. A seminar on India and South-East Asian countries was organized in Delhi by ICCR in 1966. M.C. Chagla, in his inaugural address, said that he welcomed the idea that in 'each of the Southeast Asian Countries, there should be Chairs of Indian Studies and Southeast Asian Studies and in every University we should have provision for the study of Southeast Asian Studies'.[36] The Rapporteurs' Report on the discussion on cultural development referred to suggestions in three broad categories. 'First, collaboration between Universities in the academic field; secondly collaboration between institutions within the region which are active in cultural work; and thirdly, greater exchange of information in terms of books and other material.'[37] The seminar made a number of recommendations on cultural co-operation and the important ones included the setting up of the Institute of ASEAN Studies in ICCR, establishing of branches in various South-East Asian capitals, development of institutional links, exchange of scholars, exhibitions of art and greater flow of information on contemporary India.[38] Some of these details will help us in reflecting on how far we have moved from 1966 to 2002.

India International Centre organized a seminar on 'India and Southeast Asia—Challenges and Opportunities' at New Delhi during 14–15 February 1994, while the proceedings were later published in book form in 1996. An action plan was drawn up for promoting intellectual and academic cooperation. Recommendations included gathering of data on current work being done on South-East Asia, adequate funding to specialists in South-East Asia, inviting leading South-East Asian scholars, conducting joint research projects, training of a sufficient number of language experts, establishing an Institute of South-East Asian Studies and setting up of Indian Studies programmes in leading South-East Asian universities. To ensure that follow-up action takes place, IIC was required to 'put together a panel of experts to have a comprehensive dialogue with appropriate partners in Southeast Asia'.[39]

I personally organized a seminar on 'India and Asean: The Growing Partnership for the 21st Century' in collaboration with the Institute for Diplomacy and Foreign Relations (IDFR) at Kuala Lumpur on 12 November 1997. The papers presented at this conference have been included in a book under the same title. An Indian participant, Professor R. Madhangopal recommended organizing of cultural festivals, film festivals, setting up ASEAN centres and Indian centres, promotion of tourist links through ASEAN–India Tourist Information Centre, creation of an ASEAN Fund, establishment of chairs in universities and student and faculty exchange programmes.[40] A Malaysian participant, Professor K.S. Nathan, in his paper also made certain concrete suggestions more or less on similar lines. These cover academic exchange programmes, setting up India study centres in ASEAN and focusing on South-East ASEAN Studies programme and linking of Indian universities with the ASEAN University Network.[41]

At the governmental level increasing emphasis is now being laid on development of cultural and other links consequent to India becoming ASEAN's Dialogue Partner in 1996. Professor S. Jeyakumar, Minister of Foreign Affairs, Singapore, in his capacity as ASEAN's coordinator for India, highlighted its importance when he made a statement in Jakarta on 24 July 1996. He said that 'as we focus on developing economic and political links, it is important that we continue to strengthen our cultural links. We would reap long-term gains, if we start, investing in strengthening our bridges now. This could be done through developing tourism, cultural, educational and other institutional links.'

Foreign Minister, I.K. Gujral, in his statement at the same forum, saw a linkage between cultural and commercial interests. He stated:

> The tremendous cultural capital that India and ASEAN have invested in each other over centuries has not been used to compliment and embellish our substantive economic and political relations. This must change. We must reactivate cultural agreements that we have with ASEAN countries. We must in the next four years undertake both high profile episodic cultural initiatives like festivals of India and ASEAN as well as establish more durable institutions for continuous cultural osmosis through setting up India Centres in ASEAN Countries and ASEAN Centres in India on the models of Nehru Centre we have in the UK, for example. In the matter of Culture, we must emphasize the classical as much as the popular modern manifestation of it—in music, films and television programmes.[42]

I.K. Gujral also promised to strengthen India–ASEAN academic and intellectual contacts, through proposals such as 'establishment of Chairs in Universities, student and faculty exchange Schemes between Centres of educational excellence, scholarships and fellowships. To begin with, we would like to launch an ASEAN-India Lecture series which would prepare the ground for setting up of an Eminent Persons Group (EPG).'[43]

INDIA'S CULTURAL DIPLOMACY IN SINGAPORE

India has been a late entrant in Singapore in as much as no formal arrangement to promote cultural relations existed between the two countries prior to the signing of the MoU on 5 February 1993 in New Delhi. This is largely due to the fact that the Singapore government was still not ready for a formal arrangement, while the cultural needs of the large Indian community were met locally, supplemented by visiting Indian groups. Various Singapore institutions, however, did provide infrastructure support on an ad hoc basis.

Singapore's interest in seeing a formal Indian cultural presence was conveyed by Prime Minister Goh Chok Tong, when he met Prime Minister Narasimha Rao at the NAM Summit at Jakarta in September 1992. He proposed the setting up of a permanent exhibition of Indian culture in the Singapore Museum to highlight the different cultural streams represented in Singapore. The Indian prime minister offered full cooperation for sending cultural exhibits.[44] This was followed by the signing of a formal MoU on 'Co-operation in the Arts, Archives and Heritage' on 5 February 1993 in New Delhi between the Singapore Minister for Information and Arts B.G. (N.S.) George Yeo and Indian Minister for Human Resource Development, Arjan Singh. This reflected Singapore's desire to seek 'co-operation with India in three areas: Economic, Human Resource and Cultural'.[45]

An MoU, unlike agreements with other ASEAN countries, is an executive instrument. It is only limited to three areas, which are of specific interest to Singapore. Professor Chakravarthi Ram Prasad has made an excellent analytical study of the first MoU signed in 1993. He sees the significance of the MoU in 'its being a government-to-government mode of contact' and the nexus it establishes between 'the traditional, socio-historical ones, and the latest economic and strategic ones'. He says that the main objective of the MoU is 'the creation of a climate of cultural awareness in Singapore to induce Singaporeans to venture into India economically with a sense of cultural familiarity by introducing non-Indian Singaporeans to major aspects of India's cultural richness'. Professor Ram Prasad sees symmetry in the economic context while it may look asymmetrical in terms of cultural exchanges. He states: 'The aim of both the governments is—Singapore businesses to go into India. One may put it this way: though talk of economic cooperation sounds symmetrical, in fact the flow is asymmetrical. Singaporean investment goes into India and India provides the market for adequate returns. Investment flows into India from Singapore and Culture flows from India into Singapore.'[46]

Singapore sees India in a new light also and would like India to become an important source of talented people, who could work in Singapore or for Singapore companies abroad—an issue that was raised by P.M. Goh Chok Tong with P.M. Narasimha Rao at NAM Summit in 1992. Senior Minister Lee Kuan Yew sees the expatriate communities playing an important role by using 'their worldwide network to extend Singapore's reach and grasp'.[47]

Prime Minister Narasimha Rao saw Singapore hosting Alamkara, an exposition titled 'Five Thousand Years of India' as 'a presentation not merely of ancient Indian civilization but a reaffirmation of the ties that bound our ancestors together. . . . And I myself carry part of your city in my own name. I am sure you cannot think of another guest so closely identified.'[48]

Two more MoUs were signed later covering the periods 1997–9 and 2000–2. The implementation of the executive programme has been satisfactory, with greater implementation of items under the sub-head 'The Arts'. Three statues (Ganesha, Nataraja and Durga) were handed over by President Narayanan to the Asian Civilization Museum during his visit to Singapore in 2000. The current MoU was also signed during the president's visit and he expressed his belief that 'these agreements will open up wider avenues of economic and cultural cooperation between India and Singapore'.[49] Leaders from both the countries are positive that a multifaceted relationship is likely to develop between the two countries to their mutual advantage. An exhibition on the Indian National Army is expected to be held soon in Singapore. Prime Minister Vajpayee is expected to visit Singapore in April 2002, continuing the momentum of high level visits.

Singapore is one of the few countries in ASEAN where the National University of Singapore has a Centre for South Asian Studies and that too an active one. The India–Singapore Colloquium is a good exercise and we need to evolve similar bilateral exercises with other countries.

PROMOTING CULTURAL LINKS WITH SOUTH-EAST ASIA

To sum up, culture will be an important variable along with the market and trade in determining the position of the country within a comity of nations. This aspect needs to be kept in sight not only by our leaders in the arenas of culture and trade, but also the politicians, planners, civil servants, the media and the academic world. We all, therefore, have a role to play when we conduct cultural diplomacy.

Cultural diplomacy in the form of a country's image would largely depend on its personality as seen by others and their perceptions of its inner and external strengths. The image of India would therefore have to be carved in India before it gets reflected abroad. Diplomats will be required to play an important role in projecting this image in collaboration with ICCR and other institutional frameworks available in India. A successful cultural diplomacy would have to aim at promoting not only 'India Advantage', highlighting the country's strengths but also seeking an understanding of 'India Disadvantage' with all its shortcomings.

Academia has become aware of the need to study culture in the contemporary context and this has resulted in the emergence of a new field, 'Cultural Studies'. The nature of such studies has, however, differed from one country to another. A need has emerged for the development of 'a theory of culture which could conceptualize culture in relation to other social processes within a political perspective guided by the traditional humanist values which have guided political theory in the modern period'.[50]

The role of cultural diplomacy in promoting understanding among different cultures has become more pronounced, when events are moving in the direction of clash of civilizations. This role becomes still more pronounced for multilingual, multi-ethnic, multi-religious and multicultural societies in India and South-East Asia. This factor alone should bring us together in preserving our rich cultural heritage and ways of life. In his Singapore lecture, Prime Minister Narasimha Rao captured this thought beautifully.

> Changes in human destiny need a corresponding change in men's own mindset. We have to capture the spirit and quality of that equality and realize the unity of man. This is the challenge of the unipolarity, which we witness today. This challenge is an opportunity, which history does not often throw up. We miss it at our own peril. And we can capture it, through the essentially Asian ethos of compassion, harmony and a sense of sharing, where the individual and the collective entities are beautifully blended to make life a consistent whole.[51]

There is a need to protect what P.V. Narasimha Rao calls 'a mesh, interwoven with religious, ethnic, racial, linguistic and professional strands'.[52] It would be a worthwhile venture for the experts, the National University of Singapore and India International Centre to consider organizing a seminar on 'Pluralistic Societies—Their Management and Future', in the context of present-day developments. Invitees could include representatives from other ASEAN countries, besides India and Singapore.

India had recognized the importance of cultural diplomacy even prior to Independence and had set up a nodal agency, the ICCR, in 1950. The ICCR and Indian diplomats abroad, however, have shown maturity in projecting India and receiving understanding from other cultures, while executing our programmes to build bridges of understanding. We have not encountered any syndrome of an 'Ugly Indian'. ICCR, however, has to adopt a 'Performing Arts Plus' approach and pay more attention to activities other than sending cultural troupes. ICCR has already made a move in this direction as we have seen an increase in the number of distinguished visitors coming to India over the years.

Economic reforms in India have given a new boost abroad to the understanding of Indian culture and we are likely to see culture and commerce moving in tandem in South-East Asian countries including Singapore. We may now see a reinventing of the old Silk Route phenomenon.

The push to the promotion of cultural activities will also have to come through the direct or indirect participation of the business community. They will have to become patrons of culture, as the governments or their institutions can only play a limited role as catalysts or strategists through the creation of a broad framework for cooperation in the form of Cultural Agreements, Cultural Exchange Programmes or Executive Programmes like that with Singapore. We will have to formulate rules and regulations, which encourage rather than hinder participation by sponsors of cultural activities.

Cultural diplomacy does not have to be restricted to the capitals of our respective countries, which often is the case, because of a number of infrastructural or other constraints. We have to lay more emphasis on regionalization of our activities, when we talk of seminars, chairs, centres, etc. We found this approach extremely rewarding in Malaysia when we took our programmes to cities other than Kuala Lumpur. While developing a regional approach, we have to ensure that we avoid duplication.

I would not like to venture into a new set of specific recommendations, as an exhaustive list already exists on the ground beginning from 1966—at the level of dignitaries, officials as well as academicians. What we need to do is to sift these recommendations and prioritize those that are ripe for implementation and then find the necessary resources for the same. We have to acquire an 'implementation culture' and should not be satisfied at only throwing ideas, like laying foundation stones, but not moving towards building structures. We have to acquire a 'work culture' if we wish to see success in our efforts in the field of cultural diplomacy. This we have to learn from Singapore and Malaysia.

I would, however, still like to mention a few areas which need our priority attention. We still lack basic data on ourselves—names of experts, institutions, and libraries, which are involved in these India-ASEAN and India-Singapore exercises. We could start with interlinking of ASEAN libraries with Delnet in India whose headquarters are located in IIC. However, primary focus has to be on establishment of institutional linkages and exchange of scholarships/students and conducting of seminars. There is scope within the existing availability of resources of the ICCR to augment its programme of distinguished visitors and support to seminars, which could be availed of by Indian organizations.

We can still consider Chairs of Indian Studies or South-East Asian Studies but we will have to adopt a partial funding approach where we could consider supporting some of these Chairs where they already exist or where there is a need for the same. Separately, such Chairs could be set up in IT Studies, Management or Business Studies, Strategic Studies, where we could have a course on Indian and South-East Asian Studies. This course of action is suggested, as there is no demand for purely Indian or South-East Asian Studies.

We also need to encourage students undertaking studies at least for one semester in our respective countries as in this way we could cover a large number of students without incurring high expenses. Such an exchange can, however, be possible if we pay attention to recognition of universities and equivalence of degrees. We need to mount a fresh drive with the ASEAN countries as a number of new universities are still not recognized and this is affecting meaningful exchange programmes of students/research scholars, etc. We should also plan exchanges at the level of schools.

In South-East Asia we have a cultural centre in Jakarta. Cultural centres, given their limited resources, are not the best institutions to promote Indian culture in the broader sense. We have to revitalize their functions. We do not need centres at all the places and to start with we could consider giving a regional character to the existing centre at Jakarta.

We also need to consider liberal support to local bodies that are involved in the promotion of cultural activities. In Malaysia, we found this to our advantage when we supported the Sutra Theatre and the Temple of Fine Arts in their activities in that country. We have to also revise the amount of grant to the local cultural bodies, as these have become a mere pittance in the wake of devaluation of the Indian rupee. Similarly we will have to encourage Indian participation in important activities organized by local bodies. We need to recognize these cultural ambassadors of India in one or another form.

ICCR and other institutions that are involved in the promotion of cultural activities have to evolve their programmes on a medium-term basis spread over a period of three years. Ad hoc organization of activities at short-term notice results in losing the effectiveness of the programmes, as we fail to attract the right type of participants.

While we conduct our cultural diplomacy on two tracks—Track 1 and Track 2—to ensure the independence of academia, yet we have to find a mechanism where the twain shall meet. Otherwise we will end up, as in the past, repeating a similar set of recommendations when we organize seminars or colloquia. We also need to take the experts to the field, where they can interact with students and other bodies.

The weakest link in India and ASEAN relations is the inadequate media representation in India and ASEAN countries. It is strange that *The Hindu* alone has a resident representative in Singapore, while All India Radio and the other print media have withdrawn their representatives from Singapore. We do have the local Tamil language press in Singapore and Malaysia but this needs to be supplemented with the presence of the Indian mass media in Singapore and other countries. Nothing much has happened, despite I.K. Gujral's recognition 'that the media is crucial to our direct cognition and empirical understanding of each other. We have to increase our contacts and cooperation in this area involving both print and audio-visual media'.[53]

Persons of Indian origin can play an important role in promoting cultural and commercial links. Their role in Singapore and other countries is seen in a new light in the changed international scenario. They are now being treated as conduits for promoting bilateral relations, as the cultural factor is in their favour when Singapore or other countries deal with India. Foreign Minister I.K. Gujral saw an important role for PIOs and said that they could help in spreading:

> . . . enlightenment about ASEAN in India and about the new India in ASEAN. They can be initiators as well as effective channels for trade and investment flows between India and ASEAN. While Non-Resident Indians are an additional and special factor and source for augmentation of

ASEAN–India trade and investment, contribution of all communities of ASEAN will find a warm welcome in India.[54]

The India-ASEAN Lecture Series commenced in December 1996 with Prime Minister Mahathir Mohamad giving the first lecture in Delhi. A number of distinguished visitors have come and gone under this programme. We, however, have to widen the ambit and scope of this Lecture Series and need not restrict the same to the visiting dignitaries. We also have to take these lectures to the public at large and to different centres, as their messages should not be restricted to the intelligentsia located in Delhi or in ASEAN capitals.

The climate is right for us and we can reinvigorate our relationship. I would like to conclude with the words of Prime Minister Mahathir Mohamad, as these beckon us to pool our energies in undertaking cultural diplomacy for the mutual benefit of our respective countries and people. He has put the past, the present and the future in the right perspective with these words: 'The historical and cultural linkages and the existing traditional ties form the basis or foundation on which a strong ASEAN-India relationship can be built. Being Asians, both our regions share many similarities which include eastern values and cultures.'[55]

We hope that cultural diplomacy helps us in reaching a new stage in our relationship with Singapore and other countries in South-East Asia. We hope to move away from the opinion of some commentators that 'India's historical and cultural footprints dot the region but diplomatic dividends born out of these have been marginal. They merely provide a good material for the formally worded joint communiqué.'[56] The time is now ripe to reach that stage in our relationship about which H.B. Sarkar wrote in 1985, when he observed that we can now work towards that dawn of a new age, (where) a resurgent South and South-East Asia will, it is to be hoped, renew their age-old bond of cultural ties, about which prophetic utterances were made by Rabindranath Tagore, one of the greatest poets of all time, in the most poignant way in a beautiful verse in these words:

When we tied golden threads of kinship
Round each other's wrist,
That ancient token, grown pale,
Has not yet slipped off the right arm,

And our wayfaring path of old
Lies strewn with the remnants of my speech.
They help me to retrace my way to the chambers of thy life,
Where still the light is burning that we kindled together
On the forgotten evening of our union.
Remember me, even as I remember thy face,
And recognize me as thine own.
The old that has been lost, to be regained and made new.[57]

NOTES

1. B.P. Singh, *India's Culture: The State, the Arts and Beyond*, New Delhi: Oxford University Press, 1998.
2. K.C. Alexander and K.P. Kumaran, *Culture and Development: Cultural Patterns in Areas of Uneven Development*, New Delhi: Sage Publications, 1992, p. 12.
3. Lakshmi Reddy, 'Malaysia: Perspectives on Culture', paper presented at an international conference on India-Malaysia Relations, Hyderabad, December 2001.
4. Utpal K. Banerjee, 'Role of Cultural Democracy', in *Indian Democracy: Agenda for the 21st Century,* New Delhi: Foreign Service Institute, and Konark Publications Ltd., 1997, pp. 397–417.
5. Lee Kuan Yew, *The Singapore Story: Memories of Lee Kuan Yew*, Singapore: Times Editions, 1998, p. 426.
6. T.N. Kaul, *Reminiscences, Discreet and Indiscreet*, New Delhi: Lancers Publishers, 1982, p. 189.
7. B.P. Singh, 1998, op. cit., p. 52.
8. Yogesh Atal (ed.), *Culture-Development Interface*, New Delhi: Vikas Publishing House, 1991, pp. 14–15.
9. T.K. Mazumdar, 'Indian Development: Viewed Culturally', in Yogesh Atal (ed.), op. cit., p. 62.
10. Hiranmay Karlekar (ed.), *Independent India: The First Fifty Years*, ICCR/ New Delhi: Oxford University Press, 1998, p. viii.
11. Ibid., pp. 241–53.
12. Romila Thapar, 'Secularism: The Importance of Democracy', in Hiranmay Karlekar (ed.), op. cit., pp. 18-19.
13. B.P. Singh, op. cit., p. 48.
14. Ibid., p. 74.
15. Pamphlet on ICCR.
16. Bidyut Sarkar (ed.), *India and Southeast Asia*, Proceedings of a Seminar on India and South-East Asia, New Delhi: ICCR, 1968.
17. P.V. Narasimha Rao, *Singapore, India and the Asia Pacific: Forging a New Partnership*, Singapore: Institute of Southeast Asian Studies, 1994.

18. Utpal K. Banerjee, op. cit., pp. 397–417.
19. Kishan S. Rana, *Inside Diplomacy*, New Delhi: Manas Publications, 2000, pp. 144–70.
20. Pamphlet on ICCR.
21. J. Bandyopadhyaya, *The Making of India's Foreign Policy*, New Delhi: Allied Publishers, 1973, pp. 226–32.
22. Kapila Vatsyayan, 'Culture: The Crafting of Institutions', in Hiranmay Karlekar (ed.), op. cit., pp. 486–503.
23. Warsaw, Budapest, Sofia, Seoul, Port of Spain, Bucharest, Mauritius, Ankara, Brussels, Paramaribo, Moscow.
24. B.P. Singh, op. cit.
25. Second Report, Standing Committee on External Affairs, 1996–7, Eleventh Lok Sabha, April 1997.
26. B.P. Singh, op. cit., pp. 54–7.
27. Parliamentary Standing Committee Report, ibid.
28. Arun Dasgupta, 'Intellectual and Academic Cooperation between India and Southeast Asia', in *India and Southeast Asia—Challenges and Opportunities*, ed. Baladas Ghoshal, New Delhi: IIC, 1996, p. 82.
29. H.B. Sarkar, *Cultural Relations between India and Southeast Asian Countries*, New Delhi: ICCR and Motilal Banarsidass, 1985.
30. Arun Dasgupta, 'Intellectual and Academic Cooperation between India and Southeast Asia—Challenges and Opportunities', in Baladas Ghoshal (ed.), op. cit., p. 82.
31. I.K. Gujral, *A Foreign Policy for India*, New Delhi: External Publicity Division, Ministry of External Affairs, 1998, p. 223.
32. Ministry of External Affairs (MEA), Annual Report, 1970–1, p. 23.
33. Ibid., p. 26.
34. MEA, Annual Report, 1971–2, p. 32.
35. Ibid., p. 26.
36. Bidyut Sarkar (ed.), op. cit., p. 8.
37. Ibid., p. 114.
38. Ibid., pp. 123–4.
39. Baladas Ghoshal (ed.), op. cit., pp. 81–94, 119–23.
40. K.S. Nathan (ed.), *India and Asean: The Growing Partnership for the 21st Century*, IFDR, 2000, pp. 97–114.
41. Ibid., pp. 115-27.
42. I.K. Gujral, op. cit., p. 233.
43. I.K. Gujral, ibid.
44. MEA, Annual Report, 1992–3.
45. Speech by B.G. (N.S.) George Yeo, in *A Bi-monthly Collection of Ministerial Speeches—January-February 1993*, Singapore, p. 28.
46. C. Ram Prasad 'Culture and Complementarities: Implications of the Singapore–India MoU on Culture, Heritage and the Archives', in Yong Mun Cheong and V.V. Bhanoji Rao (eds.), *Singapore–India Relations: A Primer*, Singapore: University of Singapore Press, 1995, pp. 53–77.

47. Ishtiaq Hussain, 'Singapore–India Relations in the Post-Cold War Period', in *Singapore–India Relations*, 1995, op. cit., pp. 40–52.
48. P.V. Narasimha Rao Lecture delivered on the occasion.
49. Speech by President of India at a banquet in Singapore, 10 November 2000.
50. Sarah Joseph, *Interrogating Culture: Critical Perspective on Contemporary Social Theory,* New Delhi: Sage Publications, 1998, pp. 7–21.
51. Singapore Lecture, ibid.
52. Ibid.
53. I.K. Gujral, ibid., p. 232.
54. Ibid., p. 242.
55. Mahathir Mohamad, First ASEAN Lecture, New Delhi, December 1996.
56. Kripa Sridharan, in Frederick Grare and Amitabh Mattoo, eds., *India and ASEAN: The Politics of India's 'Look East' Policy,* New Delhi: Manohar/ Centre de Sciences Humaine, 2001.
57. H.B. Sarkar, 1985, op. cit.

Syed Farid Alatas

India and the Future of the Human Sciences in Asia

INTRODUCTION: THE PROBLEM OF THE IRRELEVANCE OF KNOWLEDGE

To set the stage for this discussion on the problem of the irrelevance of knowledge and the necessity for alternative discourses, consider the following quote from the author's introduction to al-Wabar's[1] classic, *The Shi'ite Ethic and the Spirit of Capitalism*:

Early attempts by the Arabs to make inroads into Europe were relatively unsuccessful. After the subjugation of the North African coast and the conquest of the Iberian Peninsula in the early years of the 8th century AD, further incursions into Europe by Arab-Berber armies appeared to have been checked between Tours and Poitiers by Charles Martel. By the 16th century, the Ottoman Turks had overrun most of Eastern Europe and their empire extended from northwestern Iran in the east to Budapest in the West. *However, both Arab and Ottoman territories throughout Central Asia, the Mediterranean and Eastern Europe came under the threat of Shi'ite heresy* which traces its origin to the 14th century.

Contemporaneous with the emergence of the Ottoman Empire in the 14th century was the founding of the Safavi Sufi movement by Sheikh Safi al-Din. His descendant, Ismail (905–30 AH/1499–1524 AD), a Turkoman from Azarbaijan, was the founder of the Safavi dynasty. In the mid-tenth century, during Ottoman attempts to centralize their control in Eastern Anatolia, Ismail took advantage of the turmoil and attempted to make inroads there. His tribal support came from a number of Turkoman tribes, the *Ustajlu, Shamlu, Taqalu, Baharlu, Zulqadar, Qajar* and *Afshar,* collectively known as the *qizilbash* (Turk. red head). What held these tribes together was an *'asabiyyah'* (Arabic for *esprit de corps*) based on the Safavi mystical order to which the *qizilbash* owed allegiance.

So successful were Ismail and his followers in Anatolia, that by the eve of his death the Shi'ites had captured most of Ottoman territories in Europe and controlled Azarbaijan, western Iran, and the Tigris-Euphrates basin. By the reign of Shah Tahm~sb I (930–84 AH*), the Turkic Shi'ite conquerors had extended the rule of Islam to as far north as the* nahr al-r~yn *(Arabic. the river Rhine[2]). Only the lands to the east of the* nahr al-r~yn *and stretching all the way south into Central Asia and Iran remained under Turkic Shi'ite rule. The regions to the west and southwest of the* nahr al-r~yn *continued to be under Arab Sunni control as in Iberia or were ruled as various Catholic, Lutheran, Orthodox and Jewish principalities as was the case in France, Italy, the Netherlands, and Western Germany. The Turkish Shi'ite domains came to be known as Eastern Eurasia.*

We now come to the question that is being posed in this book: Why had modern rational capitalism and the industrial organization of life originated in Eastern Eurasia and not in other parts of Europe or Asia? In other words, why was the spirit of capitalism, the foundation of the capitalistic organization of life, able to fight its way to supremacy against various hostile forces here in Eurasia beginning in the sixteenth century and nowhere else? The answer undoubtedly has much to do with a certain elective affinity between the spirit of modern capitalism and the Shi'ite ethic. By the fifteenth century, the Shi'ite ethic had presented itself as constituting an ascetic compulsion to be economically successful while at the same time rejecting indulgence in the material world. The worldly asceticism of a number of puritan Shi'ite sects must be contrasted to the warrior ethic of Sunni Islam on the one hand and the retreatist monasticism of the Nahraynian sects on the other, characterizing Western Eurasia by an economic traditionalism so inimical to rational capitalist order.

These circumstances present to us the possibility of a sociological theory of the origins of modern rational capitalism. Such a theory requires not only the delineation of the features of the Shi'ite ethic to reveal the affinity with the spirit of capitalism but also an excursus into Nahraynianism and Sunni Islam in order to confirm the absence of such an affinity. Let us begin with Nahraynianism.

The term nahr al-r~yn, *from which Nahraynianism is derived, denoting the Catholic, Lutheran, Orthodox and Jewish sects of Western Eurasia, was first applied by the Arabs to the Rhine river in northern Eurasia. Those who lived on either side of the Rhine were referred to as Nahraynians* (nahrayn). *It was only after the arrival of the Turks in the 16th century* AD *onwards that the term Nahraynianism gained currency in assigning the peoples of Western Eurasia, who did not convert to Shi'ism, their religious identity. Nahraynianism, therefore, was understood by the Turkic Shi'ites to refer to the unconverted natives of Eurasia.*

This is not to suggest, however, that there is no naturally occurring entity that can be designated by the term Nahraynianism. This religion consists of Catholic, Lutheran, Orthodox and Jewish sects which all trace their origins to a Europeanized rendition of the faith of Abraham. They profess one God, a personal God, immanent but yet transcendent. They believe in a common set of scriptures, variously known as the Torah, Talmud and Bible. Furthermore, all the sects of Nahraynianism are characterized by their monastic, other-worldly and traditionalistic ethos. This made it impossible for an attitude based on frugality, discipline and systematic work centred on worldly affairs to take root.[3]

Who would accept such an account on the religion of Nahraynianism? Who would even accept that there is such an entity call Nahraynianism? What is clear from the above is a number of problems that can be said to beset Eurasian Turkic Shi'ite sociology:

1. The mix of fact and fiction: for example, there is a recognition of the existence of Catholicism, Orthodoxy, Lutheranism and Judaism as well as the Torah, Talmud and Bible but these are not understood according to the self-understanding of these religions.
2. The imposition of a category, Nahraynianism, from the outside, that is, by Arab and Turkic Shi'ite scholars. This is an imposition which does not accord with the self-description of the Catholics, Lutherans, the Orthodox Church and the Jews.
3. There is an attempt to homogenize societies and communities, thereby hiding complexities. Simply stating the commonalities of the Catholics, Lutherans, the Orthodox church and the Jews veils not only the contrary self-understanding but also the variety and heterogeneity of religion in Western Europe.
4. The approach is guilty of textualism in that it attempts to understand the reality of religion in Western Europe in terms of religious texts such as the Torah, Talmud and Bible, assuming that reality corresponds to the text.
5. Stereotyping is rife as the approach essentializes and reduces Western European society of the sixteenth century to set characteristics such as traditionalism, monasticism and other-worldly asceticism, when it was quite likely that these characterized only a section of society.

We would generally be critical of such social science by pointing to its distortions, inaccuracies and irrelevance, while being conscious of its positive and useful aspects. It would be held to be problematic because it (i) mixes fact and fiction, (ii) imposes categories and concepts from the outside that clash with self-understandings, (iii) homogenizes heterogeneous entities, (iv) adopts a textualist approach, and (v) essentializes and stereotypes whole societies.

Such social science seems simple enough to refute and one may wonder whether such bad and irrelevant social science does exist in the first place to warrant our attention to the problem of irrelevance. As ridiculous as the above account on Nahraynianism may seem, in fact, such irrelevance does exist but this is in western European and North American accounts of various parts of Asia and Africa. A case in point is the study of Hinduism. The term 'Hindu' was first used in the eighth century to refer to people who lived on the other side of the Sindhus or Indus river on the Indian subcontinent (Sinha 1991: 1), a name which was imposed from the outside to encompass a wide variety of beliefs over a vast area of land. It originally had geographical connotations which had been undergoing transformation for a long time (ibid.: 2). The adherents of such beliefs did not always consider themselves as belonging to a single religious entity that we now know as Hinduism. Yet many textualist and essentialist studies of Hinduism, such as that of Max Weber (1958), subscribed to such constructed myths.

The general problem of irrelevance has been noted in the literature of the various human sciences in a number of intellectual communities throughout the world. My purpose here is not to review this literature but to reflect on Indian concerns with this problem and on why we in South-East Asia should be interested in these concerns.

INDIAN RESPONSES TO THE PROBLEM OF IRRELEVANCE

In any inventory of responses to such irrelevant social science that has emanated from developing societies India would feature prominently. Indeed, such responses have taken two general forms. One has been to understand the causes of irrelevant social science and the other has been to suggest alternative discourse as more relevant social science.

The institutional and theoretical dependence of scholars in developing countries on Western social science has resulted in an uncritical and imitative approach to ideas and concepts from the United

States and, to some extent, Great Britain, France and Germany. Whereas, the relevance of the social sciences for developing countries has been called into question (Myrdal 1957; Singh Uberoi 1968; Misra 1972), ideas and concepts of the social sciences became entrenched. For example, even though it seemed that the humanistic and less technical political economy would be relevant because it stressed the role of non-economic variables in development, it was modern economic science in the form of abstract models that established itself in much of the Third World (Pieris 1969: 439–40).

Although the leading theoretical perspectives originating in Europe and America have not always been relevant in alien milieu, their continuing presence in university syllabi and lists of references in journal articles in the non-West are testimony to the process of adaptation to the 'rules of the dominant caste within the Euro-American social science game' (Kantowsky 1969: 129).

Among the earliest to counter Eurocentric thinking was the Indian thinker and reformer, Rammohun Roy (1772–1833). Roy lived during a period of intense proselytization activities carried out by British missionaries among the Hindus and Muslims of India. Roy was critical of the derogatory attitude of the English missionaries towards Hinduism and Islam. Replying to British objections against the literary genres of the Vedas, Puranas and Tantras, Roy argued that the doctrines of the first were more rational than Christianity and that the teachings of the last two were not more irrational than what is found in Christianity (Roy 1906, cited in Sarkar 1937/1985: 622).

A little cited but very important early sociologist, Benoy Kumar Sarkar (1887–1949), systematically critiqued various dimensions of Orientalist Indology. Writing in the early part of this century, Sarkar was well ahead of his time when he censured Asian thinkers for having fallen 'victim to the fallacious sociological methods and messages of the modern West, to which the postulate of an alleged distinction between the Orient and the Occident is the first principle of science' (Sarkar 1937/1985: 19). He attacked such Eurocentric notions as the inferiority of Hindus in matters of science and technology, the one-sided emphasis on the other-worldly and speculative dimension of the Hindu spirit, and the alleged dichotomy between Orient and Occident (ibid.: 4, 18, 35). He was also critical of the methodology of the prevailing Indology of his times on three grounds: (i) it overlooked the positive, materialistic and secular theories and institutions of the Hindus, (ii) it compared the ancient and medieval conditions of India with modern and contemporary European and American societies, and (iii) it ignored the distinction between existing institutions on the one hand and ideals on the other (ibid.: 20–1).

Sarkar was very explicit about his call for a new Indology that would function to demolish the *idolas* of Orientalism as they are found in sociology (ibid.: 28–9). Although Sarkar tended to be Hinducentric in some of his interpretations pertaining to the history of ideas in India, this does not detract from his critique of Orientalism.

In 1968, the well-known Indian periodical, *Seminar,* devoted an issue to the topic of academic colonialism, which was understood in terms of two aspects. One referred to the use of academically generated information by overt and covert North American agencies to facilitate political domination of Afro-Asian countries. The other refers to the economic, political and intellectual dominance that North American academics themselves exercise over academics elsewhere (Saberwal 1968: 10).

Despite an awareness of the state of the human sciences in India for all these decades, J.P. Singh Uberoi's indictment of foreign aid is as relevant today as it was in 1968:

> The existing system of foreign aid in science, to which the internationalist notion of collaboration lends credence, in truth upholds the system of foreign dominance in all matters of scientific and professional life and organization. It is nothing but the satellite system, with an added subsidy. It subordinates the national science of the poor to the national and international science of the rich. It confirms our dependence and helplessness and will not end them. (1968: 120)

According to Saberwal (1968: 13), the 'dependence on North American sponsors is pathetic; its consequences for problem selection, research design, and modes of publication are disastrous'. The need, therefore, for alternative discourses in India was keenly felt and did result in a critical tradition of scholarship in the social sciences and historical studies. One has only to mention the early example of Subaltern Studies to realize this.

Another interesting example comes from Rabindranath Tagore's *The Home and the World* (1919). Tagore challenged commonplace notions and attempted to transcend ideas founded on an East-West dichotomy. An example of his undermining or calling into question this dichotomy can be seen in *The Home and the World.* While this is fiction it also serves to function as a theoretical reflection on history. Standard Marxist accounts would tend to view the aristocrat as oppressive and seeking to advance the interests of the old order while the patriot and nationalist may be portrayed in a more positive and progressive light. It is partly for this reason that, as Ashis Nandy (1994: 15–16) points out, Georg Lukacs' review of *The Home and the World* (1983) was highly unfavourable, being based on a Eurocentric Marxist reading of Tagore.

TEACHING IN THE SPIRIT OF ALTERNATIVE DISCOURSES

It is this critical tradition of alternative discourses that I and a colleague at the National University of Singapore have tried to bring in to our teaching. I am not suggesting that no other colleagues in Singapore draw from Indian works or experiences but I can say with confidence that these cases are extremely rare.

Turning to a more personal account, let me illustrate our concerns with Indian scholarship in the human sciences with an example from our teaching of sociological theory at the National University of Singapore. Why read or teach the works of Marx, Weber and Durkheim or other European authors long since departed to a class of Singaporean or South-East Asian students? What have the ideas of three European theorists, born in the last century in a different cultural milieu, to do with the non-European regions of the world today?

While the various calls for alternative discourses have in *theory* questioned the existing paradigms in the social sciences, they have so far been unable to displace the fundamental assumptions of specific disciplines in *practice.* The pragmatic need to reproduce disciplines such as sociology and anthropology demands that certain continuities with the past be maintained. Hence, it is not insignificant that the critique of the human sciences are confined to the professional arena (e.g. journals, conferences and other academic forums) with the participants being established scholars and not students.

The critique of the social sciences that emanated from academic institutions in Asia, Africa and Latin America tended to remain at an abstract and reflexive level. There had been several thoughtful pieces on the state of the various disciplines, raising the issue of the lack of connectedness between social science and the societies in which it was taught. But the calls to decolonize the social sciences were generally not followed by successful attempts to build 'indigenous' theories, autonomous social science traditions, delinked from the academic core of Western Europe and North America.

Neither have these calls manifested themselves at the level of teaching in the social sciences. As far as sociological theory is concerned courses on this throughout the world tend to restrict themselves to discussion and exposition of the works of Marx, Weber and Durkheim in addition to those of other nineteenth century Western scholars.

Given this scenario, my colleague Vineeta Sinha and I have attempted to deal with the issue of teaching sociological theory by way of a more universalistic approach to the study of sociological theory. This includes raising the question of whether sociological theorizing had been done outside of the bounds of European modernity. The example of Ibn Khaldun comes to mind. This would imply changes in sociology theory curricula. We have been experimenting with various approaches entailing changes in the way sociological theory is taught. Some interesting results came out of such changes which we had reported in the journal, *Teaching Sociology* (2001).

These changes involved, among other things, introducing Indian thinkers who were grappling with similar problems of emerging modernity as nineteenth century European scholars were. For example, the works of Rammohun Roy and Benoy Kumar Sarkar were taught in addition to those of Marx, Weber and Durkheim.

I followed a similar logic in another course I taught, 'Development and Social Change'. The aim of this course was to understand the different reasons for which peoples lives in so many parts of the world are affected in one way or another by poverty, income inequality, low levels of education, corruption, political oppression, and other features of underdevelopment. The complexity of the development process can be grasped from the multitude of explanations that have emerged since the nineteenth century and include those from India such as D. Naoroji who wrote at the turn of the last century (1962 [1901]) and the Indian Marxist M.N. Roy (1971 [1922]).

THE *ASIAN JOURNAL OF SOCIAL SCIENCE*

The *Asian Journal of Social Science* is a multidisciplinary academic journal run by the Department of Sociology, National University of Singapore and published by Brill Academic Publishers. The journal has been in publication since 1973 under the title *Southeast Asian Journal of Social Science.*

As a member of the editorial board of the journal, I initiated a move to have the journal broaden its focus to cover East and South Asia. In the year 2001 this broadening in focus was reflected in the name change to *Asian Journal of Social Science.* Our view is that there is much to gain from increased interaction among social scientists in the entire Asian region. While there is much of Asia within South-East Asia as a result of centuries of cultural and economic intercourse, it is also unfortunately true that there is little exchange of ideas among the scholars of various Asian societies. It is in the spirit of improving this state of affairs that we encourage submissions that deal with South and East Asia. Since the name change it is encouraging that we have begun to receive submissions from India and certainly hope that this is just the beginning of an upward trend.

CONCLUSION

In this paper, I have only been able to touch on the problem of the state of the human sciences in developing societies that was addressed in very creative ways in India. My belief is that India should be seen as an important centre of the human sciences and historical studies and that more of the works of Indian scholars should be taught in universities in South-East Asia. This should not be confined to courses on India or South Asia but should be a feature of the more theory and discipline oriented courses. Why this is not the case is, of course, part of the problem of the over-reliance on knowledge from the social science powers, that is, the United States and Great Britain. As pointed out by one South-East Asian thinker more than thirty years ago, there is an intellectual lag in the areas of social and political philosophy and one way to address the problem is to awaken interest in the ideas of Indian thinkers and reformers (Alatas 1972: 153)

NOTES

1. Muhammad ibn al-Wabar (ad 1864–1920), the fictitious Spanish Arab sociologist, who continued the Khaldunian tradition in theoretical history in Eurasia.
2. Named so after the Arabic as it was largely Arabic geographical studies which provided detailed and systematic accounts of Eurasian climate, ecosystems and natural resources.
3. The preceding sections in italics are fictitious parts of this account of what may have happened had the Turkic Shi'ite tribes actually succeeded in their quest to conquer Ottoman territory.

REFERENCES

Alatas, Syed Farid and Vineeta Sinha, 'Teaching Classical Sociological Theory in Singapore: The Context of Eurocentrism', *Teaching Sociology* 29, 3, 2001, pp. 316–31.

Alatas, Syed Hussein. 'India and the Intellectual Awakening of Southeast Asia', in Syed Hussein Alatas, *Modernization and Social Change: Studies in Social Change in Southeast Asia*, Sydney: Angus & Robertson, 1972, pp. 151–63 [reproduced from 'India and the Intellectual Awakening of Asia', in B. Sarkar, ed., *India and Southeast Asia*, New Delhi: Indian Council for Cultural Relations, 1968].

Kantowsky, Detlef, 'A Critical Note on the Sociology of Developing Societies', *Contributions to Indian Sociology*, no. 3 (ns), 1969, pp. 128–31.

Lukacs, Georg, 'Tagore's Gandhi Novel: Review of Rabindranath Tagore, *The Home and the World*', in *Reviews and Articles*, tr. Peter Palmer, London: Merlin, 1983, pp. 8–11.

Misra, P.K., 'Social Science Researches in India: Their Relevance', *Journal of the Indian Anthropological Society* 7, 1972, pp. 89–96.

Myrdal, Gunnar, *Economic Theory and Underdeveloped Regions*, New York: Harper and Row, 1957.

Naoroji, D., *Poverty and Un-British Rule in India*, Delhi: Publications Division, Ministry of Information & Broadcasting, Government of India, 1962 [1901].

Nandy, Ashis, *The Illegitimacy of Nationalism*, New Delhi: Oxford University Press, 1994.

Pieris, R., 'The Implantation of Sociology in Asia', *International Social Science Journal* 21, 3, 1969, pp. 433–44.

Roy, M.N., *India in Transition* and *What do We Want*, Bombay: Nachiketa, 1971 [1922].

Saberwal, Satish, 'The Problem', Special Issue on Academic Colonialism, *Seminar* (New Delhi) 112, 1968, pp. 10–13.

Sarkar, Benoy Kumar, *The Positive Background of Hindu Sociology*, Delhi:

Motilal Banarsidass, 1985 [first edition published in 1937 in Allahabad, reprinted in Delhi in 1985.

Sinha, Vineeta, 'Some Notes on "Temple"-Building and Image Worship in Indian Religion, in Historical Perspective', Working Paper No. 141 (Department of Sociology, National University of Singapore).

Tagore, Rabindranath, *The Home and the World*, London: Macmillan, 1919.

Uberoi, J.P. Singh 'Science and Swaraj', *Contributions to Indian Sociology* 2, 1968, pp. 119–23.

Weber, Max, *The Religion of India: The Sociology of Hinduism and Buddhism*, tr. and eds. Hans Gerth and Don Martindale, New York: The Free Press, 1958.

Vineeta Sinha

Multi-religiosity and the Secular State: A Note from Singapore

This brief paper comes from my ongoing work on religion and the secular state in Singapore. If multi-lingualism and multi-ethnicity are two core features of Singaporean social life, then multi-religiosity is a third crucial feature. Singapore, a modern nation-state, contains within its boundaries several religious groupings and communities. In public, official and state pronouncements, this religious pluralism of Singapore is very often positively promoted as a defining feature of life on the island. In reality, and as is the case with most multi-religious societies, such a situation of diversity is accompanied by a discourse that articulates the need to carefully manage a religiously plural context. Using data from Singapore, I discuss how over time, the secular state here has talked about religious diversity and the related issue of religious harmony, in an effort to 'manage' the situation. I look at some of the strategies, arguments and mechanisms that have been employed in this effort. Apart from the state, religious communities, organizations and lay persons are also engaged in such a process of managing a religiously diverse scenario. I very briefly attend to the ways in which the state and these latter parties interacted and negotiated their position in one episode requiring 'management', through a discussion of the 'Maintenance of the Religious Harmony Act', which came into effect in 1990, and was meant to 'manage' religious pluralism in Singapore through legislation.

THE END OF RELIGION?

The first point I want to make has to do with the continued and obvious relevance of 'religion' in the modern world. In 1965, Harvey Cox wrote a book entitled *The Secular City* in which he anticipated the end of religion in the modern, urban industrial era. In fact it was quite common for social scientists in the 1960s and 1970s to argue that religion had declined in value and would eventually disappear from the modern consciousness. This was explained partly by the increasing belief in, and domination of, society by the scientific and secular consciousness. The battle between science and technology was declared to be over, with science and secularism emerging victorious (Berger 1969, Hammond 1985, Jameson 1991, Martin 1990, Wilson 1976, 1982).

If we look at the events since Harvey Cox's statement, that is, since the last thirty years, it is clear that Cox's announcement about the death of religion was somewhat premature. Instead of the end of religion, what we have witnessed rather is what has been called the 'sacralization' of societal domains, seen for instance in the phenomenal religious revivalism and resurgence and politicization of religion in the modern era. Clearly religion continues to be present, visible and central both for individuals and for communities. There is plenty of evidence that today religion remains an important organizing principle, not just at personal levels but also in mobilizing groups and communities into adopting certain attitudes and engaging in specific behaviour patterns (Casanova 1994, Heelas 1998, Luckmann 1990).

The second related point is that religious pluralism or diversity is more or less a global phenomenon. Most societies today would be defined as 'multi-religious'. By 'multi-religiosity' we could mean that different religious communities exist in and occupy the same space. Different religions that have different spiritual orientations, different ways of conceptualizing divinity, are theologically different and even contradictory or incompatible. A situation of multi-religiosity means that different religious communities are brought into close contact and their members have opportunities for interaction with each other. In this context of religious diversity, there are encounters, that is, interactions between members of different religious groupings. Theoretically speaking, *religious encounters* can produce at least two types of consequences: one, a situation of *religious harmony* leading to tolerance and understanding and two, a situation of *religious conflict* culminating in tensions and intolerant attitudes and practices.

Ideally speaking, religious diversity is highly desirable if it leads to religious harmony and tolerance and there is no conflict between the different religious communities. But as we know, a situation of multi-religiosity does not automatically lead to a situation of religious tolerance and sensitivity. It has to be worked out in specific ways depending on the context.

If we look around us for empirical, ethnographic examples, most multi-religious societies have explicitly had to manage or negotiate their religiously plural contexts. Given the present scenario, the secular state has to shoulder much of this responsibility, but religious communities, organizations and individuals have also had to devise ways of managing a multi-religious context. I illustrate this exercise using relevant material from Singapore, where, over the decades, strategies and mechanisms have been employed to handle religious differences within a secular nation-state.

MANAGING A MULTI-RELIGIOSITY SINGAPORE: CIRCUMSCRIBING THE 'RELIGIOUS' DOMAIN

The setting is the religious domain in Singapore, which is by definition a 'multi-religious' society. How does this translate into practice, and with what consequences? If multilingualism and multi-ethnicity are two core features of Singaporean social life, then multi-religiosity is its third crucial component. Singapore, a modern nation-state, contains within its boundaries several religious communities and groupings. Singaporeans can readily produce common sense religious descriptions of Singapore society by naming and listing the various 'religions' in this official secular state. This noted religious diversity is not a new or recent phenomenon for Singapore. Historically, the ethnically diverse nature of its migrant population due to the input of colonial authorities produced a religiously heterogeneous population in Singapore. So we find the major religions of India, China and the Malay world represented on the island. Additionally, the importation of religions to Singapore is not a thing of the past either; it continues to occur today, in the shape of a variety of 'reform' movements and what have more recently been popularly labelled 'new age' religious movements.

Collectively, discussions about the role of religion in Singapore society through time have resulted in a particular circumscription of the 'religious' domain. The state clearly demarcated or defined what constitutes 'religion', or more properly speaking, what defines appropriate and inappropriate or illegitimate religious activity. An examination of two themes demonstrates well how the religious domain has been quite deliberately enclosed in the Singapore context: the separation of religion from formal politics and the discourse on religious harmony.

Since independence, one central element in the demarcation of the religious domain has been its complete dissociation from the realm of formal politics. The two domains have been defined as distinct spheres and their separation is rigorously policed and maintained. Most significantly, there has been a depoliticization of religion. Religious communities could exist in the new nation-state with the proviso that their followers would not 'dabble in politics'. Given the careful demarcation of the religious domain, stepping outside these boundaries into other politically relevant areas is thus considered inappropriate. Additionally, having been defined in this fashion, religion is called upon to play a central role in nation building. Religion is to meet the spiritual, moral, and ethical needs of Singaporeans and engage in educational, social and charitable work. Religion is to be a 'spiritual ballast' and a 'moral anchor' so as to counter forces of communism, materialism and Westernization due to rapid economic change.

Yet, religions are not merely expected to concern themselves with 'spiritual' matters. Wee has pointed to the 'adoption of secular, materialist, this-worldly values' (1989:7) by religious communities in Singapore. This can be seen in the various kinds of advice given to religious groups from the earliest days of independence: they were encouraged to make religious beliefs and ideology socially and politically relevant, and to change or discard outmoded religious attitudes, to be progressive so as to be of contemporary relevance, i.e. to modernize, not to hinder material or technological progress and in a word, not to interfere with the nation's economic, material and social advancement. Looking closely at this piece of advice, we see what values are being encouraged. Religion must 'fit' itself to secular values and it is needed for the socio-political and economic development of the nation, the assumption being that the 'secular' and the 'sacred' need not be in contradiction. What is privileged is national development, and religious groups are expected to place the survival and progress of the nation—a politically constructed, secular entity—at the forefront of their own agenda, necessitated by a pragmatic stance, a defining feature of the Singapore style of governance and administration (Chua 1985, 1995). One can argue that there is a certain 'secularization' of religion here. Yet, religious groups cannot engage in social critique or comment on socio-economic and political conditions in Singapore as these could be viewed as involvement with issues outside the precisely delimited religious domain.

The discourse on multi-religiosity and religious harmony again shows how the state delimits the religious domain. Multi-religiosity has characterized Singapore society from its earliest days as a colony. Soon after its separation from Malaya, Singapore's ruling elite inherited both the fact of the republic's multi-religiosity as well as the responsibility of careful consideration and management of the same. Historically, religion has been viewed as a sensitive subject and a source of potential social conflict, but none the less considered 'legitimate' for individual spirituality. A multi-religious context indicates that different religious communities with varying spiritual orientations, opinions and viewpoints exist in and occupy the same space. Ideally speaking religious diversity is socially desirable if there is no accompanying friction and conflict. In the Singapore state's discourse on multi-religiosity, religious tolerance and sensitivity are defined as being necessary for the prevention of religious polarization and sectarian strife. From the state's point of view, these following elements are undesirable for obvious reasons: excessive religious fervour, missionary zeal and religious assertiveness. A situation of religious harmony is a matter of 'national pride', not to mention a good selling point in presenting Singapore as a haven of unity in the midst of religious and ethnic differences. Again, the tie between political stability and religious tolerance and moderation is emphasized. So the state has an obvious and pragmatic interest in ensuring that the fact of religious differences amongst the citizenry does not lead to conflict which the state sees as being counter-productive to the socio-economic and political security of the nation.

From the foregoing discussion we can draw the following inferences. It is clear that in order for its position within the state to be defined 'religion' is, first of all, reified, that is, it is talked about and treated as if it were an object with an identity and an existence quite apart from the individuals or the community who constitute and sustain it. Religion is accorded an abstract generalized singularity, devoid of any particular content. Despite the presence of religious pluralism, a certain sameness is conferred on all religions in such a discourse. It is then bestowed specific qualities and functions, i.e. a certain combination of characteristic traits that are perceived to be relevant to a Singaporean context. The different religious communities are encouraged to adopt the blueprint of what 'religion' in Singapore should be. Of course, once constructed both the boundaries and the content therein have to be 'managed' if not through argument and persuasion, then perhaps through institutional means, including legislation, as seen in the recent Religious Harmony Bill passed in Parliament. This process to my mind is a distinct illustration of state invented tradition vis-à-vis religion: conscious, deliberate and rationalized.

Yet, it is clear that in the midst of religious pluralism, tensions prevail. In recent years, such instances of strains within the religious domain have led to the passing of the Maintenance of the Religious Harmony Bill (1990). This piece of legislation signals the formal separation of the religious and political domains. The government has stated its position quite forcefully, arguing that new legislation is needed to ensure that religious harmony continues to be maintained and that religion is not exploited for political or subversive purposes. Under this item of law, any leader, official or member of any religious group or institution who causes ill-feeling between different religious groups, or who promotes a political cause or carries out subversive activities under the guise of propagating or practising any religious belief can be taken to court, and if convicted, punished accordingly. What is sociologically interesting is what this legislation in fact acknowledges about religious harmony but which otherwise remains unspoken in the state's public discourse. First, the idea that religious harmony exists in Singapore but cannot be taken-for-granted; it needs to be guarded because it is fragile and delicate. Second, that since the multi-religious balance is precarious, a conscious effort and work (on the part of individuals and the state) is needed to continuously maintain it. Finally, that despite the veneer of religious harmony, there is in fact evidence of inter-religious and intra-religious tensions in Singapore. In the discourse on religious harmony, then, we see a further circumscription of the religious domain. The state's rationale for such policing is again grounded in a pragmatic stance about the stability of the nation.

In view of the events of 11 September 2001, governments the world over, particularly those with a multi-religious citizenry, have taken on a highly cautious stance vis-à-vis religious extremism and how it could potentially destabilize religious harmony in society. Government leaders in Singapore too have articulated this fear and have publicly called for greater tolerance and understanding amongst members of different religious communities. Indeed the state has been exemplary in taking a lead in this direction by openly saying that specific religious communities or individuals should not be targeted or blamed for 'terrorist' acts, and that religious stereotyping would be detrimental to the long term multiculturalism of the community. In this discourse, one also sees the privileging of the 'Singaporean' identity over other identities—ethnic, religious or communal.

Various initiatives, some proposed by the government and others by the leadership of the various religious communities here, have already been put into practice to foster such awareness and appreciation of the true nature of religions. It is further clear that the response of the Singapore government has communicated both to the citizenry and the international community its firm and non-negotiable handling of instances of religious extremism on the island. In some ways, this response is not new for Singapore, but marks the way in which the government has routinely handled the possibility of religious troublemakers on the island for at least a few decades, as I have shown here. Thus, although the passing of the Religious Harmony Bill in 1990, was inspired by a combination of internal domestic and political factors, Singapore has scored yet another first in being steadfast and unyielding in handling 'divisive' religious elements in society. Its 'authoritarian' stance then, and in the post-11 September context, in dealing swiftly and decisively with 'religious extremists' has clearly won it admiration from the international community and from many Singaporeans too. This is quite interesting given that it is precisely this style of governance that has often also led to criticism of the government. In this instance such firmness is lauded and seen to be necessary for managing a multi-religious context and for preventing religious strife and discord.

REFERENCES

Bell, Daniel, 'The return of the sacred? The argument on the future of religion', *British Journal of Sociology*, vol. 28(4), 1977, pp. 419–51.

Berger, Peter, *The Scared Canopy: Elements of a Sociological Theory of Religion,* New York: Anchor Books, 1969.

Casanova, Jose, *Public Religions in the Modern World,* Chicago and London: The University of Chicago Press, 1994.

Chua Beng Huat, *Communitarian Ideology and Democracy in Singapore,* London & New York: Routledge, 1995.

———, 'Pragmatism of the People's Action Party Government in Singapore: A Critical Assessment', *Southeast Asian Journal of Social Science,* 13(2), 1985.

Cox, Harvey, *The Secular City,* Harmondsworth: Penguin Books, 1968.

Hammond, Philip (ed.), *The Sacred in a Secular Age: Toward Revision in the Scientific Study of Religion,* Berkeley: University of California Press, 1985.

Jameson, Frederic, *Postmodernism, or, the Cultural Logic of Late Capitalism,* London and New York: Verso, 1991.

Luckmann, Thomas, 'Shrinking Transcendence, Expanding Religion?', *Sociological Analysis,* 50(2), 1990, pp. 127–38.

Martin, David, *Tongues of Fire, The Explosion of Protestantism in Latin America,* Oxford and Cambridge, Mass.: Basil Blackwell, 1990.

Sinha, Vineeta, 'Constituting and Re-constituting the Religious Domain in the Modern Nation-Sate of Singapore', in *Our Place in Time: Exploring Heritage and Memory in Singapore,* eds. Kwok Kian Woon, Lily Kong, Kwa Chong Guan and Brenda Yeoh, Singapore: Singapore Heritage Society, 1990, pp. 76–95.

Wee, Vivienne, 'Secular State, Multi-religious Society: The Patterning of Religion in Singapore', unpublished manuscript, 1989.

Wilson, Bryan, *Religion in Sociological Perspective,* Oxford and New York: Oxford University Press, 1982.

———, *Contemporary Transformations of Religion,* Oxford: Oxford University Press, 1976.

Contributors

SYED FARID ALATAS is Associate Professor at the Department of Sociology, National University of Singapore. A Malayan national he has been with the university since 1992. He has contributed articles to a number of scholarly journals, and is currently working on a book on the philosophy and sociology of social science. He is the author *of Democracy and Authoritarianism: The Rise of the Post-Colonial State in Indonesia and Malaysia* (1997).

SANJAYA BARU is Editor, *The Financial Express.* A Ph.D. in Economics, Dr. Baru has worked as senior faculty in the Indian Council for Research in International Economic Relations, University of Hyderabad, Jawaharlal Nehru University, and University of East Anglia (UK). Noted for his coverage on economic affairs as business and economics editor for major Indian newspapers, he is the author of *The Political Economy of Indian Sugar* (1990) and *Mid-Year Review of the Indian Economy 1997–8* (1997).

YONG MUN CHEONG is Associate Professor in the Department of History, National University of Singapore. His research interests include the global dimensions of South-East Asian history. Among his publications are *Asian Traditions and Modernization: Perspectives from Singapore* (1991) and *Singapore-India Relations: A Primer* (1995), co-edited with V.V.B. Rao.

AMIT MITRA, currently Secretary General of the Federation of Indian Chambers of Commerce and Industry (FICCI), is an economist with an academic background. Dr. Mitra has been addressing policy changes on many economic issues of importance in the pre- and post-liberalization era of the Indian economy.

S.D. MUNI is Professor, Centre of South, Central, South-East Asian and South West Pacific Studies, School of International Studies,

Jawaharlal Nehru University, New Delhi. He held the prestigious Appadorai Chair of International Politics and Area Studies at the School of International Studies, 1995–7. Apart from holding numerous academic and government positions, Prof. Muni served as Ambassador of India to the PDR of Laos from November 1997 to December 1999.

PETER REEVES is Visiting Professor and Coordinator of the South Asian Studies Programme at the National University of Singapore. Emeritus Professor of South Asian History at Curtin University (Perth, Western Australia) and Fellow of the Academy of the Humanities in Australia, Prof. Reeves' current research is on the history of fisheries in colonial and post-colonial South Asia and the politics of economic liberalization in West Bengal. His publications include: *Sleeman in Oudh* (1971), *Ports and Port Cities as Centres of Social Interaction in the Indian Ocean Region* (1981), and *Landlords and Governments in Uttar Pradesh: a study of their relations until zamindari abolition* (1991). Prof. Reeves was the Co-Convenor of the Second India–Singapore Colloquium.

PARAMJIT S. SAHAI retired from the Indian Foreign Service. He served as Ambassador/High Commissioner to Malawi, Lesotho (1981–4), PDR of Yemen (1988–90), Sweden (1992–6) and Malaysia (1996–2000). He also served in the Ministry of Commerce; was posted as Minister of Commerce and Supply in Washington DC (1984–7) and Deputy Chief of Mission with personal rank of Ambassador to the USSR (later the Russian Republic) during 1991–2.

BILVEER SINGH is Associate Professor in the Department of Political Science at the National University of Singapore. His research interests focus on security issues in South-East Asia. His published works include *The Vulnerability of Small States Revisited: Singapore's Post-Cold War Foreign Policy* (1999), and *ASEAN, the Southeast Asia Nuclear-Weapon-Free Zone and the Challenge of Denuclearisation in Southeast Asia* (2001).

JASJIT SINGH, Air Commodore (retd.) is Director of Centre of Strategic & International Studies, and former Director, Institute of Defence Studies and Analyses, New Delhi. He has been Visiting Lecturer in defence and war colleges in India and abroad, and has

published extensively on strategic and security issues. Among his more than three dozen books are *Non-provocative Defence* (1989) and *India's Defence Spending: Assessing Future Needs* (2000).

VINEETA SINHA is Assistant Professor at the Department of Sociology, National University of Singapore. She is also Deputy Editor of the *Asian Journal of Social Science* and on the Academic Editors panel of the *Asian Social Science Series*. Her current research interests are in the field of comparative Sociology of Religion and Hinduism in the diaspora.

KRIPA SRIDHARAN teaches in the Department of Political Science, National University of Singapore. She is the Book Review Editor of *Asian Journal of Political Science*. A regular contributor to academic journals on issues of foreign policy, comparative regionalism and Indian foreign and domestic politics, she is the author of *The ASEAN Region in India's Foreign Policy* (1996) and has co-edited *Human Rights Perspective* (1999).

FAIZAL BIN YAHYA is Assistant Professor in the South Asian Studies Programme at the National University of Singapore, and was a member of Singapore's International Environment and Policy Department (IEPD) of the Ministry of the Environment. He is currently writing a book on Singapore-India trade relations and has published two research papers on India and Singapore in the *Asian Studies Review* (1995).